In Our Darkest Hour:

HOPE

Our Journey with
Guillain-Barré Syndrome

BRIAN L BEEKS

WESTBOW
PRESS®
A DIVISION OF THOMAS NELSON
& ZONDERVAN

WestBow Press books may be ordered through booksellers or by contacting:

WestBow Press
A Division of Thomas Nelson & Zondervan
1663 Liberty Drive
Bloomington, IN 47403
www.westbowpress.com
1 (866) 928-1240

ISBN: 978-1-5127-5833-7 (sc)
ISBN: 978-1-5127-5835-1 (hc)
ISBN: 978-1-5127-5834-4 (e)

Library of Congress Control Number: 2016916385

Print information available on the last page.

WestBow Press rev. date: 10/21/2016

To our son, Benjamin, whose life has been shaped for the good because of his GBS journey, and to my wife, Bootsie, who is my partner in life and in ministry.

Contents

Forewords

Straight talk from those who have come through some of life's great challenges will always be treasured—and their courage admired. Life holds few more challenging tasks than parenthood. This remarkable book is written from a truthful heart and is helpful, encouraging, and educational—especially concerning Guillain-Barré syndrome.

In Our Darkest Hour: Hope is a powerful demonstration of passing through tough, discouraging times without a "Do as I say" stance, but rather saying, "Here is what happened and here is how we survived—and ultimately thrived."

Faith, prayer, and spirituality play very personal and key roles in *In Our Darkest Hour: Hope*. In our dark hours, our best human instinct is to seek hope and to open our hearts. Seven words of Samuel Beckett come to me: "I can't go on. I'll go on." These are also quoted by the dying Paul Kalanithi in *When Breath Becomes Air*.

My own healing crises passed when I learned through experience how my thinking impacts my healing: as long as I kept telling myself I was ill, I remained so. It wasn't until I changed my thoughts and prayers to those of healing and health that I indeed became healed and healthy.

It has been my privilege to work with Pastor Brian Beeks by doing some editing on this manuscript. I can easily visualize anyone sharing this heartwarming book with any family members or friends who face their own challenging times.

Jo Ann Lordahl
Writer

It's been said that everyone experiences a train wreck at some point in life. We all hope that the train wreck will happen to someone else—that our smarts or abilities or planning or resources will protect us, keeping us immune from the troubles and difficulties of life.

Well, even if that's how we hope life will unfold for us, eventually we learn that we have been living in a bubble of denial and make-believe. Every one of us, at some point or another, suffers heartaches, illnesses, setbacks, or defeats. In fact, many people are surprised to discover that Jesus *promised* that hard times would arrive. The night before His crucifixion, He made this statement to His followers: "In this world *you will have trouble*. But take heart! I have overcome the world" (John 16:33, emphasis added).

And so troubles are not optional—but our response to trouble is.

I have known Brian and Bootsie Beeks nearly forever. My wife, Sandy, and I were the matchmakers who introduced our best friends to each other. And over the years, we have seen their delightful son, Benjamin, grow into a strong, confident, Christ-centered young man.

In the pages that follow, you will read about how a rare disease threatened to shred their lives and relationships into unrecognizable tatters. You will also learn how their faith was stretched, challenged, and strengthened. Their story is one well worth knowing and reflecting upon. Their journey inspires all of us who dare to venture out in genuineness and faithfulness.

Kris McPherson
Spiritual Care Coordinator with Heartland Hospice
Fort Wayne, Indiana

Preface

When our son was hospitalized, I had been a United Methodist pastor for more than twenty years. I had walked with numerous families through life-and-death crises. My son's illness made crisis much more personal.

The challenges families and caregivers face when a loved one deals with an extended illness and recovery took on a new level of significance for me. As we faced our challenges as a family, I sensed a prompting within my spirit that we would need to share our story with others—not only those who share the same diagnosis as our son, but especially those with extended hospital stays and long recoveries.

At first, I thought the book would be a collection of short devotionals that also described our journey, but as I began writing, the narrative unfolded more logically as a story that includes spiritual reflections.

This is not intended to be a medical textbook about Guillain-Barré syndrome, but it is a description of our experiences and our understanding of what we went through.

I began writing this book about five and a half years after our son's initial diagnosis. Time has helped us to evaluate some of the lessons we learned. We were able to recall many details because my wife journaled for several weeks until it became too painful for her to continue. We also reviewed email communication as well as medical records. When reviewing these documents, we were surprised by the intense emotions we relived.

It is my desire that through the story of our journey, others might be able to find hope in their darkest hour.

Acknowledgments

I would like to thank the people of Monticello United Methodist Church who loved, cared for, and nurtured me and my family through our difficult journey. The church was also gracious enough to work with me to develop a three-month sabbatical for my wife and me in the spring of 2015. The sabbatical allowed me to step away from my responsibilities at the church so I could reflect, process, and write about our journey as a family.

The sabbatical was underwritten through a generous grant to Monticello United Methodist Church by the 2013 Lilly Endowment Clergy Renewal Program for Indiana Congregations, funded by the Indianapolis-based Lilly Endowment Inc. and administered by Christian Theological Seminary. This was one of the twenty-two awards made to Indiana congregations in August 2013. I am very appreciative and humbled that I was able to be the benefactor of one of these grants.

I want to give special thanks to the church staff who not only supported us on our journey when our son was recovering, but also took on additional responsibilities when I was away on my sabbatical.

Thank you to Jo Ann Lordahl, who acted as my writing coach and primary editor, helping me to tell our story in a compelling way. I also appreciate the numerous people who have read the story at various stages in the writing process and have given their suggestions and encouragement.

Throughout the book, the names of doctors and hospitals have been changed, with the exception of our son's pediatrician, Dr. Thomas Padgett, Peyton Manning Children's Hospital and Home

Hospital in Lafayette, Indiana. Home Hospital closed a few months after Benjamin's hospitalizations because of hospital mergers and new construction. Peyton Manning Children's Hospital played a special role in the story, and its significance would have been lost with a name change. We appreciate the work and concern of all the doctors and medical teams who worked with us, but we can never adequately thank Dr. Padgett and the staff at the Pediatrics Associates of Lafayette for their patience and compassion.

Finally, I would like to thank my wife, Bootsie, and my son, Benjamin, for allowing me to tell our story. This was a tough journey for all of us. Bootsie carried much of the load as she dealt with the ever-changing challenges. I don't know how I could have made this journey without her.

As a family, we agree that this is not a season of our lives we would ever want to relive, but I am proud of who Benjamin has become, and I appreciate his willingness to allow the details of our journey to be told.

Introduction

The hard knocks of life are no respecter of persons. I had been a United Methodist pastor for twenty-two years. My wife, Bootsie, and I had been married for seventeen years. Our only son, Benjamin, was thirteen years old. We'd had challenging seasons in our lives, but nothing compared to the journey we were about to take.

Some people erroneously believe pastors and their families live in a protective bubble and don't face problems like other families. The truth is, pastors and their families don't receive special exemption.

Others believe pastors are uniquely equipped to deal with challenges that others might not be able to handle. I won't deny that faith was an important component of our journey, but my faith isn't unique because I'm a pastor. Pastors face struggles, heartache, and challenges, just like everybody else. Members of our family get sick, and those illnesses can cause permanent disabilities or even death. Members of our families aren't miraculously shielded from depression and emotional disorders. And the hard knocks of life can cause a crisis of faith.

I'm a person of faith. I want to live as a person of faith, but that doesn't mean I always live my faith or express it perfectly. When I have doubts, it is a reflection of where I am at that moment. A doubting thought or a doubting action doesn't mean I have abandoned faith; it means I still have room for growth.

The pages that follow tell the story of our family's journey and our particular crisis of faith.

Chapter 1

Just Suck It Up

It was a typical Sunday morning. I was up at six to review the details of the worship service. Bootsie and I ate breakfast at seven thirty, and by eight, I'd headed to the church. It was about nine when Benjamin got up to shower and get ready.

After showering for a few minutes, he pounded three times on the floor, a thud heard throughout the house. This was the usual household signal for anyone upstairs to get the attention of someone downstairs. His mother went to the door of the bathroom. Benjamin was a thirteen-year-old prepubescent boy, and of course we respected his privacy, so she cracked the door open and asked him what he needed.

He said his legs felt weak, so he'd sat down in the shower. And he was so weak he couldn't get up. Benjamin asked her to come in and help him out of the shower. So she helped him up and over to the toilet to dry off.

This was unusual, but kids get sick and weak sometimes. Bootsie told him to stay home from church and rest so he could be ready for school on Monday.

After church, Bootsie and I returned home. Benjamin didn't feel any worse, but his legs were still weak. He didn't move from the couch except to go to the bathroom. As he went to bed that night, he leaned on the hallway wall for support. We assumed he'd be back to normal in the morning.

As we started our Monday morning routine, Benjamin continued to complain of weakness in his legs. We dismissed it as growing pains and weren't concerned. At breakfast, he said, "Can you write a note to my teachers in case I can't get between classes in time?"

This seemed like an unnecessary and crazy request. "Just suck it up," I told him. "Push yourself. You can surely get between your classes in the five-minute passing period."

His mother told him she'd call the doctor to see what he thought. She expected the doctor's response to be "just watch him for a couple days, and if anything changes, let me know."

Bootsie took Benjamin to school before eight o'clock, a little earlier than usual, so she could give the office staff a heads-up about his weakness. She told them she'd give the doctor's office a call. If the doctor wanted to see him, she'd return to pick him up for the appointment.

At home, Bootsie called the pediatrician's office and explained to Dr. Padgett's nurse the events of Sunday morning and that we'd sent him to school this morning. She added that Benjamin said his legs felt weak and somewhat numb.

The nurse not only wrote down what Bootsie said, she also noted that Benjamin had received a nasal-spray flu vaccine just nine days earlier. That notation had a greater significance than we knew at the time.

The nurse said Dr. Padgett was doing rounds at the hospital and would be in when he finished. She didn't indicate any reason for immediate concern. When the doctor arrived in the office at around nine thirty that morning, his nurse shared the content of Bootsie's phone call. His response: he wanted to see Benjamin immediately.

The nurse called Bootsie and asked, "How soon can you have him here?" She replied that it would take about an hour. She'd have to call the school, get him out of class, and make the forty-five-minute trip from his school to the doctor's office in Lafayette, Indiana.

The fact that the doctor wanted to see Benjamin immediately didn't set off alarms, as Bootsie assumed he had an opening at the beginning of his office hours and was fitting Benjamin in first. She called the school to tell them she'd pick up Benjamin. Then she called to let me know.

We were conscientious about Benjamin's health, but even with the pediatrician's request to see him, we weren't overly concerned. He was a healthy boy. He was very active. This was a problem that would undoubtedly pass quickly.

Before Bootsie could sign him out of school, the office had already notified his classroom teacher. Benjamin came down the hallway, using the wall for support as he walked.

When they arrived at the doctor's office, the nurse immediately escorted them into an exam room. From the very beginning, the doctor must have thought he knew the diagnosis. However, he didn't mention any possibilities.

Instead, he asked Bootsie, "So what do you think it is?"

Because it's so easy to be an "Internet doctor," making your own diagnosis before ever seeing a professional, he may have been fishing to find out what sort of research she'd done.

"I have no idea," she replied. "That's why we came to see you."

Dr. Padgett checked Benjamin's strength and reflexes and then walked him down the hallway and back. Benjamin shuffled as the doctor looked on.

Next he sent them across the street to Home Hospital for X-rays of Benjamin's back and hips, along with some lab work. They'd return to the doctor's office for results at one thirty that afternoon.

The doctor wrote "stat" on the tests, but still Bootsie felt no anxiety about anything being seriously wrong. She assumed the doctor wanted the results back for their one-thirty appointment, and the only way to ensure quick results was to mark them "stat."

While they were still at the hospital, my wife called the church office to let me know Benjamin was getting X-rays and lab work. They'd see the doctor again after lunch. We talked, but there was nothing to share other than what they were doing. She promised to keep me posted.

When they returned to the doctor's office, the X-ray and lab work were normal. The next step was an MRI, so they returned to the hospital. As they walked to the registration desk, Benjamin's eyes focused on an empty wheelchair. As he tried to get his mother's attention, a staff member, seeing Benjamin's struggles, asked, "Would you like to use a wheelchair?"

"Yes," Benjamin said, and he took a seat.

They wheeled him to the MRI. Although he had never had an MRI, he wasn't afraid. Actually, being in that tube surrounded by construction-like pinging noises intrigued him. When the test was over, he joined his mother in the waiting room. The technician called the doctor's office with the results, and they waited for instructions of what to do next.

After about thirty minutes, the receptionist asked my wife to talk with the doctor, who was waiting on the phone. Dr. Padgett said the MRI looked normal, but he wanted to admit Benjamin to the hospital for a twenty-four-hour observation. He also wanted a neurologist to examine him.

Up until then, neither my wife nor I had been overly concerned, but the new developments raised red flags. Two visits to a doctor's office and two rounds of tests at the hospital, and nothing in the way of even a preliminary diagnosis—this wasn't a good sign.

Bootsie called me around three thirty to say Benjamin would be admitted to the hospital. She had a packing list of things for me to bring to the hospital for their overnight stay. I left the office immediately, went home to pick up the requested items, and left for the hospital.

Benjamin reported to the pediatric unit of Home Hospital in Lafayette. His room, considered private, was furnished with two beds and a long, cushioned bench seat. The window looked out over Columbian Park just across the street. His was probably the largest, most spacious room on the floor. Of course, we had no idea how many days Benjamin and his mother would spend there over the next two months.

The nurses were caring and compassionate. They knew how scary hospital admissions can be for children and their families. Benjamin, like most people, wasn't fond of needles. The nurses did their best to explain what they were doing and to calm any fears and anxieties.

As the day progressed, the strength in Benjamin's legs continued to decrease. By the time the nurses did their intake assessment, even standing as they weighed him was a struggle.

After office hours, Dr. Padgett came in. He didn't have any new information, but as I'd now arrived, he explained none of the tests had shown anything unusual. The referred neurologist, Dr. Nuckols, would see Benjamin that evening. After the doctor left, we asked the nurses what time Dr. Nuckols usually made rounds. "Between six and midnight" was their answer.

For ages, a person who is in the hospital receiving care has been called a "patient," because those who are ill are expected to be patient while they await care. From the very beginning, our practice of patience was challenged. We just wanted some answers.

At about seven in the evening, a nurse said Dr. Nuckols was on the pediatric unit. His initial neurological exam lasted thirty minutes. Everything was new for us, but eventually the neurological exam would become routine.

From head to toe, the doctor did a thorough exam. Although most results were normal, he paid special attention to strength and reflexes as he assessed Benjamin's legs, ankles, arms, hands, and fingers. Alarmingly, when the doctor tested Benjamin's knee reflexes, his lower legs did not respond.

After the neurological exam, the doctor wanted to do an electromyelogram (EMG). The test couldn't be done in Benjamin's room, so we took him to another floor for it. Benjamin's nurse found a wheelchair, and we all followed the doctor to the EMG lab.

The lab wasn't much larger than an oversized closet, but Dr. Nuckols invited us to join him for the test. The EMG was a very unpleasant and painful experience for Benjamin. It involved measuring the responsiveness of certain nerves in his legs and arms to electrical stimulation.

The doctor began by placing two needles in Benjamin's leg. Then, through the needles, he administered various levels of electrical shock. The test measured how much time it took the electrical stimulation to move along his nerves. This process was repeated on multiple nerves in each leg as well as in his arms.

The test itself was painful, but the anxiety and the anticipation of being shocked with increasing intensities of electrical current made the agony worse. It was torture watching our young son endure this misery. Aware that the testing was necessary, however, we had to accept the process. The EMG lasted about an hour, though it seemed to stretch much longer.

At the conclusion of the test, we returned to Benjamin's room. The doctor went to the charting area of the nurse's station on the fourth floor. By about nine, he returned to share his diagnosis. Unfortunately, the EMG study wasn't conclusive. He wanted to repeat it the next day. His conclusion, based upon his neurological exam, was that Benjamin had Guillain-Barré syndrome (GBS).

Chapter 2

A Whole New World

Even the sound of the phrase *Guillain-Barré syndrome* was ominous. And I'd never heard of it. All Bootsie remembered from her nurse's training was that GBS patients ended up on a ventilator. After hearing the diagnosis, she couldn't focus on anything more the doctor said. And I struggled to understand.

Guillain-Barré syndrome is an autoimmune disorder where a person's body fights against itself. Beginning with the longer peripheral nerves in the legs and arms, the disorder moves toward the trunk. A myelin sheath, which Dr. Nuckols compared to the plastic coating on an insulated wire, covers the nerves in the body. With GBS, the myelin sheath is eaten away, causing muscle weakness. The nerves can mend, but nerves heal much slower than other parts of the body.

At that point, only Benjamin's feet and legs seemed to be affected, and Dr. Nuckols said GBS would probably progress to his hands and arms. Stopping this progression was vitally important. Otherwise, it could affect Benjamin's breathing. Compromised breathing would require a ventilator.

We asked the neurologist how a person gets GBS. He explained that it's uncertain. Also uncertain is why one person gets it and another person doesn't. Some people contract GBS after having the flu or after an infection in an open wound. He added that GBS is a rare side effect of certain vaccinations. As Benjamin had just received a nasal-spray flu vaccine nine days prior to the onset of symptoms, Dr. Nuckols assumed the vaccine was the most likely trigger for his GBS.

"There are two standard treatments," he told us. "Plasmapheresis and intravenous immunoglobulin, or IVIG." Plasmapheresis is a process of cleansing the blood similar to a dialysis treatment. The patient's blood is filtered through a machine that separates the plasma from the blood cells. The blood cells are returned to the body while the plasma is replaced with a saline solution. This rids the blood of unhealthy antibodies thought to cause the immune system to work against itself. An IVIG is an intravenous treatment in which the patient is given healthy antibodies from blood donors. Both of the treatments have equal success rates. If treatment starts with plasmapheresis, IVIG can't be utilized. However, if IVIG isn't successful, plasmapheresis is still a possibility.

The doctor's parting words were "I'll be back tomorrow. You can let me know which treatment you'd prefer."

As the doctor left, Bootsie barely held back her tears. All she could visualize was her only child on a ventilator. I struggled to understand what it all meant, but I was optimistic because of the early diagnosis and treatment options. Initially Benjamin didn't show much emotion, but later he confessed to being scared. There was much he didn't understand, but what he could grasp petrified him.

It wasn't long until the nurse came to carry out the doctor's orders. She explained what she was doing, and she added that lab work in the morning would mean drawing blood.

Even though Benjamin wasn't experiencing breathing problems, the potential of compromised breathing concerned the doctor. Respiratory therapy would check every eight hours to evaluate his vital capacity, a measure of how much air he was taking into his lungs. As long as his lung capacity didn't decrease, there was no reason to be concerned about GBS affecting his breathing. If

Benjamin's vital capacity began to decrease, however, a ventilator might be necessary.

A pulse oximeter was placed on his finger to constantly monitor oxygen levels in his blood. It was a contoured clip that lightly gripped his finger like a clothespin. It had a red light that glowed through his finger, and since we had to find some way to lighten up, that became known as his ET finger. A little bit of humor provided a means for us to dispel some of the stress and anxiety we were experiencing.

Four electrodes connected to his upper body via sticky pads constantly monitored his heart rate and rhythm. Twenty-four hours a day, these rhythms showed on a monitor above his bed and at the nurse's station.

Extra precautions were imposed. Benjamin's condition could worsen and affect his ability to empty his bladder. So his bladder would be scanned at least once every shift after he went to the bathroom to see how much urine remained. The nurse also told Benjamin that he was a fall risk, so he should never get out of bed without a nurse or one of his parents helping him. A final instruction was that a physical therapist would work with him daily.

An overnight stay in the hospital hadn't sounded so threatening, though the doctor's diagnosis had been a bit overwhelming. Now, as the nurse began implementing the doctor's orders, the seriousness of our situation began sinking in. It became frighteningly clear that this would no longer be just a twenty-four-hour admission to the hospital.

At about ten thirty, all the activity began to quiet down, and we started thinking about sleeping. The nurse told Bootsie that she could use the second bed in the room. We decided that I would go home for the night, stop by the office in the morning, and then return to the hospital.

Before I left, we prayed together. "Lord, we thank you for the doctors and for their quick diagnosis," I said. "We pray that you would give us and the doctors wisdom as we decide the best treatment. We pray for healing to come to Benjamin's body and that we would find your grace to be sufficient during the time of recovery. We pray for a good night's rest. Through Jesus Christ our Lord, we pray. Amen."

After I left, Bootsie turned off the lights, got into bed, and turned away from Benjamin so he wouldn't see her crying. After a few minutes, Benjamin broke the silence, "Mom, am I going to die?"

I can only imagine her feelings, though I understood her fears and the uncertainties ahead for the three of us. More concerned than Benjamin, I'm sure, she comforted him, assuring him he'd be all right and that death was a long way off.

Benjamin slept well the first night in the hospital. But his mother didn't. Between nurses coming in every two hours to check on Benjamin and her mind going a hundred miles a minute with questions and fears of the unknown, she was awake more than asleep.

Chapter 3

Understanding GBS

At six the next morning, Bootsie showered and dressed for the day. Then she began researching. With no Internet access, she phoned a family member who was a nurse practitioner, seeking to learn more about GBS, IVIG, and plasmapheresis.

Our pediatrician, Dr. Padgett, visited at about eight on that Tuesday morning. He said he had suspected GBS, but the neurologist was the one who had to make that diagnosis. He reminded us what was at stake and that many times GBS affects a patient's breathing.

Dr. Nuckols had left the pediatric floor at about ten on Monday night, and to everyone's surprise, he returned to the floor at ten that morning. On the one hand, it was good to see the neurologist before his evening rounds. But a morning visit indicated his concern and reinforced the severity of the potential diagnosis.

When Dr. Nuckols came to Benjamin's room to check on him, an intern, Dr. Timothy, accompanied him. Dr. Timothy, doing a pediatric rotation, listened intently as once again Dr. Nuckols explained GBS. First he drew a picture of a nerve with the myelin sheath and explained how the patient's own body destroys the sheath. He also delineated again the merits of plasmapheresis and IVIG, recommending five treatments of IVIG. Bootsie agreed, since that would still leave the option of plasmapheresis. Dr. Nuckols also wanted to do another EMG.

It was Dr. Timothy's last week on the pediatric floor, and he was experiencing a diagnosis that many doctors wouldn't personally encounter in a lifetime of practicing medicine. So, after Dr. Nuckols left, he went to the medical library and searched the Internet for more information. He found a couple of helpful articles and copied them for Bootsie to read. During this first admission, he served unofficially as Bootsie's personal research assistant.

Because Benjamin's illness had a possible connection with receiving a vaccination, the doctor was required to make a report to the Centers for Disease Control and Prevention (CDC). It was called a Vaccine Adverse Event Reporting System report (VAERS). So, on November 10, 2009, Benjamin's symptoms, type of vaccine received, and the lot number of the vaccine was reported to the CDC.

A frustration for me, and perhaps for the doctors, was that the VAERS report appeared to be a one-way street. The doctor was required to share information with the CDC for their database, but the CDC shared nothing in return. I couldn't help but wonder if other teenagers in the fall of 2009 had had the same reaction to that vaccine. Was this indeed a rare occurrence, as the doctors said? Or was something else happening with that year's flu vaccine? We wondered if Benjamin's dose came out of a bad batch.

It was very frustrating not to get solid answers. I was feeling very much out of control as a parent. I had always been able to care for my son's needs, and now I felt helpless. The CDC and medical professionals say, "You need to get a flu shot." But when there's a complication, *the system* doesn't seem willing to communicate what they may know.

Let me be clear; we were very pleased with Benjamin's medical care and the doctors and nurses who worked with him. My frustration with the CDC came because they never shared information with us—except a denial of any connection between the vaccine and Benjamin's condition.

When a minor receives a seasonal flu vaccine or any other vaccination, the parent or legal guardian must sign a consent form. On the form, in small print, are all the known side effects. In the case of the flu vaccine, GBS is one of those possible complications. After the diagnosis, the doctors said that for every one million people who get the flu vaccine, one person will contract GBS, according to statistics. Benjamin was lucky (unlucky) enough to be that one in a million.

I wanted to understand why Benjamin had contracted this disorder. I didn't believe there was any doubt in the doctors' minds that the cause was the flu vaccine, but the CDC wasn't willing to assign responsibility to the vaccine.

The CDC is concerned about public health. Their recommendations are based on what they believe to be the best practices for the most people. Those with GBS normally recover, but twelve out of every million who have the flu die from it. There is no known recovery rate from death. I can't verify the statistics, but anecdotally, you're more likely to die from the flu than you are from contracting GBS because of a flu vaccine.

When people heard Benjamin's story, they'd ask, "Does that mean I shouldn't get a flu shot?" Even though Benjamin was advised against receiving another flu vaccine, we tell people the risks are greater and more catastrophic without the vaccine than with the vaccine. We can't find statistics that compare GBS rates for the nasal-spray flu vaccine versus the injection, but Benjamin received the nasal mist because of his phobia of needles. I don't know anyone who loves needles, but sometime during his hospitalizations, his fear of needles disappeared.

Bootsie had taken Benjamin for his vaccine on October 30, 2009. She signed the consent form for him to receive it. After his diagnosis, the fact that she'd signed his consent form brought a heavy load of guilt that she was somehow responsible for his condition.

Of course, she didn't sign the consent form with any malicious intent. She was the one available to take him for the shot, and I certainly didn't object. The CDC and medical professionals advised parents that giving their child a flu vaccine was the responsible thing to do. Logically there was no reason for her to feel guilty, but guilt isn't always logical.

Dr. Nuckols ordered the first IVIG treatment for Tuesday, and it took a couple of hours for the pharmacy to prepare the prescribed dosage. When the nurse brought the treatment into the room, it was a clear liquid that didn't look any different from the bag of saline solution already hanging by his bedside.

Several possible side effects were associated with IVIG treatments. Because of those side effects, when the treatment was infused, his nurse monitored him very closely, checking his vitals every fifteen minutes.

When Dr. Padgett came in after his office hours on Tuesday, we asked about the expected recovery time for Benjamin. He said that though most patients have a full recovery, nerves heal very slowly, so we were probably looking at eighteen months. While we trusted him, we'd never heard of anything taking so long to heal. We reasoned, "He is a young growing boy. He's a runner and in good shape. Benjamin will heal much quicker. Life will be back to normal before eighteen months."

An interesting thing we discovered about GBS is that patients are often misdiagnosed at least once or twice before the correct diagnosis is made. This means a misdiagnosed patient may go several weeks without appropriate treatment. We were optimistic that since Benjamin had a correct diagnosis from the very beginning, his recovery would be quicker. That conclusion sounded logical, but things don't always turn out as one might think or hope.

All day on Tuesday, Benjamin talked about and dreaded the repeat EMG. When Dr. Nuckols arrived in the evening for the test, Benjamin attempted to use his power of persuasion to talk him out of doing the EMG. It didn't work; the doctor insisted it was needed to confirm the diagnosis.

When three or four of the nerves were tested, Dr. Nuckols found what he'd expected. The time it took the electrical shock to travel down the nerve had increased. This supported the diagnosis he'd made based on clinical observations the night before.

When Benjamin was admitted to the hospital, we'd notified the church prayer chain, but until the diagnosis was confirmed, we didn't share anything. After the neurologist's visit on Tuesday evening, we began to share the diagnosis of GBS and to ask people to continue to pray.

We'd never known anyone with GBS. However, after the diagnosis, we started hearing the stories of others whose lives had been touched by it. A member of the church who received the prayer chain update stopped by the local radio station. She knew the owners of the radio station had had their own journey with GBS several years earlier, so she told them of Benjamin's diagnosis.

In the prayer chain email, we'd given people permission to share Benjamin's diagnosis. The more people we had praying, the better. Not only was his name included on the prayer list of many local churches, but his name was also added to prayer lists across the nation.

I don't know whether the radio station shared Benjamin's name on the air Wednesday morning, but they asked the community to pray for a thirteen-year-old boy in the Monticello community who'd been diagnosed with GBS.

Kevin and Laura, the owners of the radio station, reached out to us, as did others whose lives had been affected by GBS. One of Benjamin's former teachers had the chronic form of GBS, and he called Benjamin after receiving our permission. A complete stranger from South Carolina who once had GBS called because he'd heard about Benjamin through his church's prayer chain. I don't fully understand, but there seems to be a connection with any individual or family who has had his or her own GBS journey.

On Wednesday, Benjamin's condition continued to deteriorate. The tingling and weakness he'd experienced in his legs had spread to his arms. When Dr. Padgett came in that morning, he once again reminded Bootsie of the possibility of the GBS affecting his breathing. "You know, if he needs to be put on a ventilator, we will need to ship him out of here," he said. With no pediatric intensive care unit (PICU) in Lafayette, Benjamin would be transferred to a larger hospital with a PICU ventilator. Dr. Nuckols was adamant that if the vital capacity of Benjamin's lungs started to be impacted in any way, he wanted him transferred immediately.

A physical therapist came to Benjamin's room every day to work with him. On Tuesday, they had him stand independently from a sitting position on the side of the bed. As the week progressed, he was able to do less and less.

As Thursday got started, it was shaping up to be the worst day yet. As Benjamin awoke that morning, he'd wet the bed and had a very painful headache. They were already doing a bladder scan every shift, because they were concerned the GBS might progress and he wouldn't be able to empty his bladder completely.

Our doctors had indicated that GBS was sometimes extremely painful. At the time, we didn't know exactly what that might mean. We were thankful Benjamin had had little pain up to that point. He'd experienced only a tingling sensation in his feet and legs and now in his hands and arms. Bootsie's first thought was that he was now entering the painful part of the disease.

On Thursday morning, when the doctor came in at about eight, Benjamin was lethargic. His speech was slurred, and he was unable to walk with a walker. He was dragging his feet, was losing bladder control, and was nauseated.

Benjamin was crying. Bootsie was crying. The doctors and nurses were worried because everything pointed toward a progression of the disorder. Respiratory therapy was called to assess his vital capacity. As the doctors had warned, if his breathing began to be compromised, they'd immediately transfer him to another hospital.

The nurses closed the blinds because he was so sensitive to light. They gave him something for his pain, and he went back to sleep.

Once all the commotion in the room calmed down, Benjamin was sleeping, and my wife sat helplessly by his bedside, crying. She texted me around nine to tell me that they weren't having a good morning and that I needed to come to the hospital right away. She also texted others, asking them to pray.

Bootsie was handling the minute-by-minute details of things happening in the hospital. Even though she hadn't practiced nursing for nearly fifteen years, she was more familiar than I was with hospital procedures and working with the medical staff.

Her maternal instincts required that she stay physically close to our son. I was obviously concerned, but I also had a full-time job. I had responsibilities at the church, but I also had some flexibility as to when and where those obligations would be completed. I was at the church office most mornings and then would head to the hospital in time to pick up lunch. I returned to the church for any evening duties. Otherwise, I'd work at the hospital on my laptop and utilize my cell phone as much as possible.

Of course, I was involved with Bootsie in making major medical decisions, but one of my major tasks was providing emotional strength for my family. Bootsie vented to me, releasing her fears and frustrations. Sometimes I helped give her perspective when her vision was narrow. I was also the one who talked with Benjamin and tried to encourage him to take a more positive perspective. I was at the hospital as much as I could be. When not at the hospital, I was on call, prepared to come at a moment's notice.

That day was one of those days when everything felt overwhelming for Bootsie. I was needed at the hospital.

When I arrived about ten, Bootsie met me in the hallway and said, "He just woke up, and he's doing fine." Fine was relative, but his headache was gone, and he seemed to be doing as well as he'd done the day before.

On Thursday evening, after completing his third IVIG treatment, Benjamin's condition began to improve. We and the doctors breathed sighs of relief. He struggled to walk with a walker, but with assistance he could once again make it between his bed and the bathroom.

We were sustained by faith, but we also gave thanks for the wisdom and knowledge God had given the doctors. We believe all truth is God's truth. The level of knowledge and wisdom medical professionals possess is because God allows the truth of His creation to be revealed. We also believe in the power of prayer. Some would say that consulting doctors and praying are inconsistent, but I believe they are complementary.

From a medical perspective, the migraine was a side effect of the IVIG treatment. The other physical concerns on Thursday morning were cause to believe that Benjamin's condition was worsening. From a faith perspective, we believe we experienced answered prayers on that day.

Chapter 4

Feelings of Isolation

The doctors told us we should expect a minimum of five or six days in the hospital. There was a time when weeklong hospital stays were commonplace, but not anymore. During Benjamin's stay on the fourth floor, we saw a revolving door of admissions and dismissals. Most patients were there only overnight.

Most hospitalizations involve a patient who is sick and doesn't feel like having company. In Benjamin's case, yes, he was sick, but he wasn't contagious. He was also awake and alert. Social stimulation was a positive thing. As a culture, we don't have a practice of visiting people in the hospital, and we often don't know what to do or say.

Benjamin's need for socialization was further challenged by the restricted visitation policy. At the time of his admission, the number of flu cases was on the rise. The CDC was on high alert for an outbreak of H1N1. Because of the heightened concern, the Lafayette hospitals, along with many other hospitals across the state of Indiana, were limiting visitors. No one under the age of eighteen was allowed to visit anyone in the hospital, and the number of visitors in a room was limited. Doctors were also very concerned that Benjamin not contract H1N1, which could exacerbate his condition.

Yes, we understood the reason for the restrictions, but Benjamin didn't see any reason why exceptions shouldn't be made for him.

Many adult visitors gave us support, including visitors from our church, family members, and friends. They also interacted with Benjamin, which was good. Yet as the days wore on, he was becoming discouraged over not interacting with his peers. Over the course of the week, twenty or so balloons and many cards surrounded his bed, which was testimony to the support and concern of others. Still Benjamin's feelings of being isolated were rising.

After the turnaround on Thursday, things began looking up. The doctors had said Benjamin would receive five IVIG treatments, which meant he'd receive the fifth treatment on Saturday. We were hopeful he'd be released on Saturday or Sunday.

On Saturday, Dr. Nuckols wasn't satisfied with Benjamin's level of strength. The neurologist instructed that his body be given a day off on Sunday. Then he'd receive one more IVIG treatment on Monday.

After his sixth IVIG treatment on Monday, we were ready to go home. Seven nights in a hospital were enough for both Bootsie and Benjamin. Everyone looked forward to having the family back together at home.

The events of that week had been overwhelming, with a lot to process and so much we didn't understand. We needed to focus on healing and physical therapy so Benjamin could get stronger. Doctors advised us that the damage to the nerves was already done. It would take many months for those nerves to heal. The doctors also warned Bootsie and me about possible complications.

Everyone's hope was that the series of IVIG treatments would facilitate Benjamin's full recovery. IVIG didn't really "heal" GBS; it slowed the progression and decreased its severity. It was possible that the symptoms would return within the next two to three weeks. If they did, the doctors would consider whether he had a chronic form of GBS, called chronic inflammatory demyelinating polyneuropathy (CIDP).

I'd equipped Benjamin's bathtub with a handheld showerhead and bath bench so he could sit down to take a shower independently.

To get upstairs, he would sit on the steps and move himself one step at a time. He'd make the trip downstairs only once a day and then back up at the end of the day. This slow process was also a source of physical therapy.

We tried to establish an exercise and homework routine. On Friday, after his Monday discharge from the hospital, Benjamin started doing physical therapy at a nearby office. He wasn't thrilled about going, but at least he was more cooperative with the therapist than he was with his parents.

The physical therapist at the hospital gave him a page of exercises he should do each day. It would be a long process, and exercise was a key part of his recovery. Nevertheless, he always had an excuse. He was too tired, which was true. Tiredness is natural with GBS, but inactivity only makes the tiredness and weakness worse. Doing his exercises became an escalating household battle. Beyond the concern over the GBS recovery, the emotional tension was rising over his lack of motivation to exercise and his lack of social interaction.

After about a week at home, the battle over exercising blew up. It was Sunday afternoon. Benjamin was already upset because the doctor had said he couldn't go to church. He didn't want him in a crowd where he could possibly pick up H1N1 or some other virus that might be present in a public gathering of people.

When Bootsie tried to get Benjamin to exercise, he yelled at her in frustration, "It doesn't do any good. I'm not getting any better." Barely holding things together emotionally, she left the room to cry. I was at the church with a class I was leading, so I couldn't referee or act as a buffer. I was later told it was a silent and tense afternoon around the house.

On Sunday evening, church friends came to play games with Benjamin and to allow us to get out of the house. This was Bootsie's first opportunity to get away from home with me since the hospital discharge. Everything felt so overwhelming. Was he over GBS or not?

We were still in the two-week window when doctors said symptoms could return. As a nurse, even though she hadn't practiced for about fifteen years, Bootsie knew how important it was to follow doctors' orders. When Benjamin refused to do his exercises, she didn't know how to motivate him. It seemed she wanted him to get better more than he wanted to get better. She could do only so much.

Sunday had been a horrible day. Benjamin went to bed, presumably to sleep, at about seven that evening. At eight, he called his mother on her cell phone and said, "We need to talk." The events of the day had been symptoms of his concerns and fears. He cried for about an hour, actually sobbing in a fetal position. Finally, he was releasing emotions he'd bottled up for the past two weeks. When he finally calmed down and could talk, he said, "I've never thought of suicide before. Recently I have. But I'm not stupid enough to do that."

When it came to schoolwork, Benjamin's teachers were very understanding and willing to work with him. He had always excelled in school, but we noticed he wasn't as mentally sharp as before his hospitalization. I worked with him on algebra homework, but it was a slow process. Mentally, he just wasn't able to concentrate and focus as he once did. Was this a result of the GBS? Was it because of lack of motivation? Was it because of depression? The answer to all three questions was probably yes.

Each day got a little bit longer. Benjamin desperately wanted to go where his friends were, and they weren't accustomed to coming to the house before he got sick. School and church were his main points of interaction with his peers, but these were the two places the doctor didn't want him to go. His next doctor's appointment was on the last day of the month, which was still over a week away.

As the days wore on, Benjamin begged Bootsie to call the doctor and see if he could at least go to school at lunchtime to see his friends. We weren't sure how the school would view that idea, since he wasn't attending classes. Benjamin finally wore Bootsie down, and she called.

Dr. Padgett reiterated his concern about Benjamin being in a crowd of people. He did agree to allow Benjamin to go to Sunday school. But he said he shouldn't go to the worship service, with its larger crowd and potentially more germs. He also gave Bootsie a heads-up that when they came for his appointment next week, he might not clear Benjamin to return to school.

Bootsie also talked to the doctor about Benjamin's emotional state, and he asked if she wanted him to prescribe a mild antidepressant. His question caught her a little off guard, and her immediate answer was no. "Let's give it a little more time before we take that step."

Bootsie wasn't sleeping well. When she went to bed, she'd relive the frustrations of the day. She'd feel angst and frustration with a child who wouldn't do what he needed to do to get stronger. Words had been said that couldn't be taken back. There was also emotional wear as she was with her son 24/7, and the guilt of taking Benjamin to the doctor to get the vaccine remained. Fears and what-ifs ran through her head. *What if he isn't over this? What if he has the chronic form?* Restless nights didn't help her get the rest she needed to face the next day.

Whenever visitors came to the house, they'd find Benjamin sitting on the couch, watching TV or playing video games. The most common comment when we walked a visitor to the door was "He looks so good."

He did look good. He looked like a normal teenager sitting on the couch. When a person saw him struggling to walk with his walker or to go up and down steps, it was obvious not everything was normal.

During his first week at home, Bootsie vented her fears and frustrations to a friend by email: "He looks good, and I know at some point someone (middle schoolers probably) will say he's just faking this because he looks so good. The damage has already been done, and no one can see that damage."

When she wrote those words, she had no idea how profoundly those fears would be realized.

Chapter 5

Here We Go Again

As Sunday morning arrived, Benjamin was excited. He could finally get out of the house and go to Sunday school. In the twelve days since the hospitalization, the only time he'd left the house was to go to a doctor's appointment or to physical therapy. If I could motivate him, we'd go for a walk outside.

The doctor was very specific: Benjamin shouldn't be out in public places. We enforced the doctor's orders, but his mother took the brunt of his anger over the restriction.

Benjamin was thirteen. He didn't understand why the doctor didn't want him out in public. Besides that, as an only child, he was rather self-centered. He wanted what he wanted and would do everything possible to make life miserable for anyone who stood in his way.

Bootsie took him to church just in time for the beginning of Sunday school. He went in the main door, took the elevator to the basement, and went directly to his class. He was thrilled to see his church friends. And as soon as class was over, his mother took him home.

At lunchtime, Benjamin talked about his experiences in Sunday school. "About halfway through the class, my feet and legs started to tingle," he said. Bootsie and I heard, but we tried not to overreact.

We downplayed it as much as we could and encouraged him that everything was all right.

After an afternoon nap, Benjamin continued saying his legs felt weak and were tingling. When we attempted to elicit more description, he said it wasn't the same feeling as when your leg or arm "goes to sleep," but he didn't know how else to describe it. It wasn't a painful feeling. He just knew his legs didn't feel right.

While Benjamin and I sat on the couch to watch the Colt's football game, his mother went in the other room to call the pediatrician. She explained that we weren't seeing any changes, but Benjamin was describing a different feeling in his legs. The doctor said to watch him, and if it got any worse, to take him to the hospital.

We sat on the couch, cheering on the Colts. When the game was over, I got up to sit at the kitchen table. Benjamin had a science project due. (Actually, because he was so far behind in his classes, I knew the project was probably late. But his teachers were gracious and understanding about his schoolwork.) He was to build a bridge out of Popsicle sticks so it would support the greatest amount of weight. He'd started building the bridge. Our goal was to get it finished that afternoon.

Motivating Benjamin to focus on homework was a challenge, and I thought I'd found a window of opportunity. When one of those windows presented itself, it was important to act.

Benjamin tried to get up from the couch to use his walker, but his legs gave way. I jumped from the kitchen table into the family room to catch him before he hit the floor. After the fact, Benjamin laughed about the incident, saying he didn't believe he'd ever seen me move as fast as I did that afternoon.

We realized we needed to return our son to the hospital. Immediately Bootsie called the pediatrician. He said to go directly to the pediatric floor, where his team would be waiting.

We never did get that bridge completed.

We arrived at the pediatric unit by five thirty. This visit wasn't as scary as the first one. There was certainly the fear of what everything meant, but the medical procedures and equipment were no longer unfamiliar and therefore not as overwhelming. The nurses called Benjamin by name with a smile and welcomed him back to the floor. As they wheeled him down the hall, they extended hospitality by saying, "Benjamin's suite is ready and waiting." He had the same room where, just two weeks earlier, he'd spent seven days.

The on-call doctor was in contact with the neurologist. Dr. Nuckols instructed him to begin another series of IVIG. Around eight, they got the IVIG treatment started, which meant all the other precautions and monitoring was started as well. They checked his vitals every fifteen minutes during the infusion.

Just twelve hours earlier, Benjamin had been getting around with a walker. Now he couldn't even stand independently. Additionally, he noticed the feeling in his arms he'd earlier felt in his legs. Though they brought a bedside commode for him to use as a toilet, I had to lift him out of bed and sit him on it.

This sudden deterioration was troubling. It raised many questions. Did we do the right thing by allowing Sunday school earlier in the day? Was he not past the destructive stage of GBS when he was sent home? Did overexerting himself cause the physical manifestations of the GBS to return? Was this a recurrence? Did he have CIDP, the chronic type of GBS?

We had many questions but no definite answers.

Medically we were doing all we could for Benjamin. And we continued to rely on our faith. Bootsie sent an email to the church prayer chain as well as to those who'd been following Benjamin's progress and praying during his first hospitalization.

As the GBS symptoms were on the move again, a major concern was that the disease might spread to the nerves in his diaphragm muscles and lead to breathing difficulties. So as his mother asked for prayers, she asked people to pray that the progression would stop and that he wouldn't need to be placed on a ventilator.

The symptoms were more severe this time than last and were progressing faster. It was frightening to watch.

I left the hospital late that night, probably after ten thirty. The IVIG treatment still had another sixty to ninety minutes before it would be completed. Back to our old routine, we prayed together as I prepared to go home. My wife spent the night at the hospital, and I returned home to sleep and to try to keep up with things at home and at the church.

Benjamin was a trooper and seemed to be taking things in stride, but we knew he took his lead from us. If we were upbeat and confident, so he was too. If we showed fear and anxiety in front of him, he'd notice it. His mother, of course, was a support for him and oversaw his medical care. As a mom, she needed to be near her son. She couldn't even think about leaving him in the hospital by himself.

When the IVIG treatment was finished, they went to bed. Benjamin slept some that night, but when things quieted down, the emotions of the day began to catch up with Bootsie. When Benjamin was asleep, she could let her guard down. She was an emotional wreck most of the night. The fear of how far things would deteriorate haunted her. He was already worse than he'd been at his lowest point during the previous hospitalization. He couldn't move his legs. He couldn't reposition himself in bed. He did have some feeling in his legs, but he just couldn't move them.

When Bootsie wasn't worrying about how bad he would get, she stressed about managing things at home when he was released. How could we get him around the house? His bedroom was upstairs, so how could we get him up and down? Where could we put his bed? Benjamin had also been uncooperative about exercises and therapy after the last dismissal. How would she handle him at home? There was a seemingly endless list of concerns to worry about.

The people of the church understood, and the church staff was supportive, but I couldn't just drop all my responsibilities. I had some vacation time, but I hated to use all of it up. The doctors had told us recovery was a long road, so we didn't know what the future held.

During this time, we gained a new level of empathy for parents with chronically ill children. How do they care for the needs of their child while also keeping up with work and other family responsibilities? How do single parents do it?

We were fortunate. Bootsie wasn't working outside the home, so she didn't have to choose between going to work and being with her son. Benjamin was an only child, so we didn't have other children to care for and to support. My hours were flexible. I could do some of my work on my computer at the hospital, and I was available by cell phone. I did my best to keep up with all my responsibilities. As I look back, I'm not sure how we survived. It was certainly a season I don't wish to relive. On the positive side, I believe we became more sensitive to families who face these types of struggles.

I tried to arrive in the office before eight in the morning to do what needed to be done. Then, between eleven and eleven thirty, I'd head to the hospital. Normally my wife had texted me a list of things to bring from home, and I'd try to pick up the items on the list and the mail before I left. Cards received in the mail were a highlight of Benjamin's day.

I'd often call on my way to the hospital to see what they wanted to eat for lunch. I'd pick up lunch, not only for Bootsie, but also for Benjamin. The hospital food was good, but he was a picky eater, and food wasn't a battle we chose to fight. He had no dietary restrictions, so if he felt something sounded good to eat, I'd get it.

Dr. Padgett did his hospital rounds at about eight, before his office hours. On his Monday morning examination, Benjamin had trouble sitting and maintaining balance. Because he was dependent upon others to move him in bed, Dr. Padgett ordered compression hose. These were a flexible vinyl material held around his lower legs with Velcro straps. The material would fill and deflate with air, helping to prevent blood clots. He also ordered a special blow-up mattress to minimize the risk of bedsores.

Because we'd been through this once before, Bootsie assumed everything would be the same, and that when released from the hospital, Benjamin would go home. Now we learned that, following this hospitalization, Benjamin would need to go to a rehabilitation facility. When the doctor mentioned that, it was actually a relief. After a sleepless night, this would solve many of his mother's concerns.

As the doctor left the room, he motioned for Bootsie to follow him into the hallway. That was unusual; he normally said whatever he had to say in front of Benjamin. He said Dr. Nuckols, the neurologist, would be in later and would probably want to do another EMG and possibly a spinal tap.

"Why?" Bootsie asked defensively before breaking down in tears. If they already knew it was GBS, why did they need to repeat the EMG? And why was a spinal tap necessary? Dr. Padgett didn't give her a reason, she told me later, at least not one that registered when she was so worried and upset.

When Dr. Nuckols came on Monday afternoon to examine Benjamin, he conducted his neurological assessment as he'd done daily in the last hospitalization. This routine was so familiar; he almost didn't need to tell Benjamin what to do next. The doctor assessed reflexes and strength and did a neurological workup.

During the first hospitalization, there had been discussions of a relapse and the possibility of a chronic form of GBS called CIDP. It was still too early to make a diagnosis of CIDP, but it couldn't be ruled out. Benjamin was very anxious about having the chronic condition. Quite naturally, he feared he'd be dealing with this nightmare the rest of his life.

We didn't know how to describe what was happening to Benjamin other than to call it a relapse. But Dr. Nuckols said he wouldn't consider it a relapse. While it seemed much longer, it had been only three weeks since the initial onset of symptoms. Even though he had hoped the previous IVIG treatments would get Benjamin beyond the time when GBS was actively attacking his peripheral nerves, we were still in the period when the doctor considered it a continuation of the first onset, not a relapse. The treatment would be another round of five IVIG infusions.

Dr. Nuckols was noncommittal about how long it would take the IVIG treatments to stop the progression again, and he was unable to tell us how far the GBS would progress, since it affects each person differently. It wasn't that Dr. Nuckols didn't know what he was doing; it was simply that no one could answer the question with certainty. What he did say with certainty was that Benjamin would be "out of here" if his breathing began to be compromised. Again, he was referring to the possibility of Benjamin being transferred to a hospital with a PICU.

Chapter 6

※━╋━※

Struggling to Pray

Thankfully Benjamin wasn't in pain. He just couldn't move independently from the waist down. Going to the bathroom was probably the most difficult aspect because of the loss of privacy. When I was present, I'd cradle him in my arms and carry him to the bathroom. I sat him on the toilet and then helped him stand to his feet. While I was bearing most of his weight, his mother pulled his pajamas down, and I sat him on the toilet. When he was finished, we'd reverse the process, and I'd carry him back to bed.

Of course, Benjamin preferred I take him to the bathroom. But when I wasn't there, a nurse would help his mother get him on a bedside commode. I guess you do what you have to do, and you chalk it up to one of the indignities of being in the hospital.

Benjamin couldn't walk, but he was pretty upbeat spending most of his day in bed. He was thankful for a steady stream of visitors, as they helped pass the time of day. Even though he appreciated the adult visitors, he was frustrated because visitors under the age of eighteen still weren't allowed to be in any patient's room.

Benjamin's physical and emotional needs were at odds. Physically it was vitally important he not contract H1N1. But emotionally he needed interaction with his peers.

He had received his own cell phone on his thirteenth birthday. Staying in contact with his friends through texting was important. Bootsie's phone was very basic. She couldn't email from it, and up until then she'd done very little texting. But texting became a good way for her to communicate and may have helped her maintain her sanity. I was concerned that she too was feeling isolated from friends—and maybe even from me. We never seemed to have time, or opportunity, to talk about anything except Benjamin's care.

Whenever I arrived at the hospital with my computer, Bootsie would check her emails, trying to stay connected with life outside the walls of Benjamin's hospital room. Emails became a good place to get information to those who were interested; it didn't require making multiple personal contacts or responding to the same questions from many different people. When a family is walking through a health crisis like this, it's helpful to have a public forum where information can get out to interested people without having to make numerous contacts.

People take many different approaches when a loved one is in the hospital. Some are very private and don't want anyone to know what they're experiencing. They don't want others to know because they themselves are coming to terms with the diagnosis or condition. Others share too many details. I don't think there's one right way to respond. We chose to be open.

Since I was a pastor, numerous people knew about Benjamin's hospitalizations. Many were concerned and praying for all of us. We wanted people to pray for us, and they could pray more specifically if they knew what was going on. Unfortunately, rumors and gossip can also come into play. If we didn't choose to share information, something would fill the void. That void could easily be filled with something other than the truth.

Benjamin's health consumed his mother 24/7, and outside of my church responsibilities, his illness consumed the rest of my time and energy too. When interacting with others, with the people of the church, and with the staff, I wanted to be transparent enough to let people know what we were walking through. But I didn't want to overwhelm them with too much information. This was sometimes a difficult balance to strike.

On Tuesday morning, Benjamin experienced some shortness of breath. There'd been so much concern about the possibility of breathing problems and being placed on a ventilator, when anything at all changed with his breathing, the nurses went on high alert. This of course raised the stress and anxiety level for Bootsie.

Benjamin's nurse called respiratory therapy. A therapist came immediately to measure his vital capacity—that is, the volume of air he was inhaling and exhaling. The respiratory therapist said everything was fine. Nothing had changed. There was a collective sigh of relief, but they continued to monitor his breathing a little more closely.

Dr. Padgett had told Bootsie that Dr. Nuckols would probably want to do another EMG. But she didn't say anything to Benjamin. Dr. Nuckols didn't mention an EMG on Monday, but on Tuesday afternoon, he stated his intentions of doing another. Benjamin was dealing with all the medical procedures pretty well, but another EMG was far more than he was prepared to tolerate. He came unglued. He was adamantly against a repeat of that painful procedure.

My wife, of course, had told me about her conversation with Dr. Padgett on Monday, so I had a little time to prepare for Dr. Nuckols's request. As a parent, I was torn. Benjamin had gone through a lot; I needed to be his advocate. But if another EMG was medically necessary, I didn't want to do anything to interfere with his care. I said to the doctor, "We know what this is, so why another EMG? If the test won't provide any new information—other than confirm what you already know—why put him through the test again?"

Dr. Nuckols heard my concern, but as he left the room, he didn't say whether he'd do the EMG or not. Benjamin appreciated my advocacy but stayed on edge, worrying about the doctor's decision. Thankfully, when the doctor returned a couple hours later, he said he'd wait another day. If Benjamin started improving by the following day, it wouldn't be necessary. Bootsie immediately sent out an email asking people to pray for improvement.

When Dr. Padgett made his rounds on Tuesday evening, Benjamin stood and took two tentative steps. It wasn't major progress, but it was an indication that the deterioration had possibly stopped.

On Wednesday, there was significant improvement. His legs were stronger, although not as strong as his weakest point during the first hospitalization. But he could stand for one minute with the help of the walker and two physical therapists. This was huge. After no voluntary movement from the waist down for over two days, it was such a relief to see movement returning.

Was Benjamin's improvement an answer to prayer? Or was it a result of the IVIG? There was no way of knowing, but I choose to believe the answer was yes on both accounts. We and many others had prayed that Benjamin's condition would stop deteriorating, and it did. We also prayed the IVIG treatment would be affective.

I have faith in God. I also believe God works through the knowledge and truth he has revealed about the human body and medications to scientists and medical professionals. I always want to walk by faith, but I believe it would be foolishness to ignore medical science and only pray. And the prayers of others gave us the strength and support we needed to endure. Prayer was a vital part of our journey with GBS, and I believe it made a difference.

It's impossible to quantify the significance of prayer. To be honest, it was hard for us to pray for ourselves. This is when the prayers of others became so important. In Exodus 17 is a story of Joshua leading Israel's army into battle. Joshua was on the front lines with the fighting men, but the outcome of the battle didn't seem dependent upon him and the Israelite army. It was dependent upon Moses, who stood on a mountainside, overlooking the fight below. Whenever Moses' hands were raised, Israel's army had the upper hand and was winning. But when Moses' hands were down because he grew tired, the Israelite army faltered and seemed on the edge of defeat.

When Moses grew tired, two of his assistants, his brother Aaron and a man named Hur, helped him. The Bible tells us Aaron and Hur brought a stone for Moses to sit on. It doesn't say they moved Moses to a place where he could sit down on a stone. No, Aaron and Hur brought a stone. We don't know the details of what the stone looked like, but if it was big enough for Moses to sit on, I'd guess it was a heavy stone. Aaron and Hur would have had to do some heavy lifting to bring the stone to Moses. Then as Moses sat down, the story continues, the two men held Moses' hands up for him.

When Moses was too weak to hold up his own hands, Aaron and Hur did it for him. This is how we'd describe the role of those who prayed for the three of us during our GBS journey. When we grew weary and could no longer make it on our own, others held us up. We felt the spiritual strength of those who prayed for us.

People supported us in many ways. Get-well cards for Benjamin as well as notes of encouragement for us as caregivers were very important. A gift card to a restaurant near the hospital was an appreciated act of kindness. We can't begin to describe how much visits in the hospital and at home meant to all of us. These were all sources of encouragement and strengthening during our journey. We believe God used others to hold us up and support us when we were too weak to do it on our own.

When life is disrupted, normal activities stop. When illness or tragedy strikes, it's a definite change in life. Suddenly, your regular activities are put on hold or may even cease altogether. For example, my wife took a break from her many volunteer activities in the church. My schedule changed as well, but I continued to have work responsibilities. I spent less time in the office and delegated more responsibility to staff. I attended every meeting where my presence was needed, but I mostly sent my regrets where my attendance wasn't essential. Thanks to cell phones and Internet, I was able to stay in touch with the office when needed.

Bootsie left the hospital on only a couple of occasions when someone Benjamin was comfortable with would come and stay with him. She and I would use the time to go to a local restaurant and talk. One of the toughest things for us as a couple was that we had no time together, and when we did, it was always consumed with talking about Benjamin's needs and issues.

That's what parents do; they care for the needs of their children. I'm not complaining, but one of the major struggles when you have a seriously ill child is that every hour of your day is consumed by the illness. Even when I was working, it was ever-present in my subconscious. At night it often shaped my dreams or would keep me from falling asleep.

We had a strong marriage, but we began to understand why marriages break up when there's a family crisis. We had no time, or maybe we took no time, to nurture our relationship. We were both just trying to survive the crisis. There was never any point during our journey when I thought our marriage would break up, but there were certainly times when I thought life would be easier if I could just bail out of the situation. I gained a new understanding of how someone might want to escape a relationship, especially if the marriage wasn't strong before the crisis hit.

Benjamin's life came to a halt. He loved school, but he couldn't attend. He enjoyed youth activities at the church, but the doctor didn't want him in crowds. Besides that, he couldn't move independently as he could just a month earlier.

Our life was turned upside down, but we attempted to maintain as much normalcy as possible. Benjamin needed to find a way to continue certain things. One of those was his schoolwork. He began feeling more and more overwhelmed as the unfinished homework accumulated. Logically, if he were stressing over homework, you would think he would at least work on it. But he didn't. Even though he appeared to interact with people normally, the GBS apparently affected his ability to think and process information. Learning wasn't as easy for him as it had once been. It took much more effort to learn new concepts than it had prior to GBS. Homework began to pile up. Benjamin's response to the stress was to avoid homework, which only made things worse.

All of his teachers were patient and extended grace on late assignments. His algebra teacher, Mr. Casey, and his communications teacher, Ms. Obholz, each came to visit him during his first hospitalization. Those visits gave Benjamin a sense that he was still connected at school. Mr. Casey went over and above what we'd have expected by tutoring him in the algebra lessons he was missing.

During the second hospitalization, Mr. Casey offered to include Benjamin in their algebra class every day through Skype. This technology is now commonplace, but at the time, the middle school had never used it. Nor had the hospital pediatrics department ever had a patient connect with a class over the Internet. It was extra work for Mr. Casey, but his offer to Skype the algebra class was a diversion from the normal hospital routine and was a way to keep Benjamin connected at school, which he was really missing.

Until then, my wife had access to her email only when I brought my computer to the hospital, so we'd talked about a laptop computer for both her and Benjamin. She had been feeling more isolated with every passing day. Another argument for a laptop was that when Benjamin did return home, getting him upstairs to the family computer would be a major undertaking.

Mr. Casey's offer to Skype algebra was the final piece that convinced us to get a laptop. Hospital staff was intrigued by the whole idea. Beyond Benjamin's medical care, they also wanted to do what they could to help him stay connected at school. The administrator of the pediatric unit talked with the hospital's IT department to help us work out details.

Wednesday was the first day for Benjamin to join the algebra class by way of the Internet. Nurses were very accommodating, working with physical and respiratory therapy to ensure Benjamin was uninterrupted during his algebra class. On the first day, he could connect to the class with audio but not video. This technical glitch was worked out in a day or two. For all the disruptions GBS brought to Benjamin's life, the Internet was a way to maintain connection and normalcy for his learning—at least in algebra.

Even though Benjamin was less mobile than he had been at his previous lowest point, he showed signs of improvement. This welcomed relief was the motivator to begin pursuing the next step. Dr. Padgett had said Benjamin would go to a rehabilitation unit when dismissed from the pediatric medical unit. He had only two IVIG treatments remaining, so his mother began researching pediatric rehabilitation units. She could find only two in our area, if you consider a hundred-mile radius to be our area: the Bippus Hospital for Children (BHC) in Chicago and Peyton Manning Children's Hospital (PMCH) in Indianapolis. Both were about ninety minutes from where we lived.

When she called BHC, she learned they didn't have a pediatric rehab unit. It had been a premier pediatric hospital for years, so the idea that they didn't have a pediatric rehabilitation unit was hard to believe. Besides, information on the hospital website said they did. So Bootsie wouldn't let the switchboard operator's answer end her pursuit. After she persisted and insisted, the operator transferred her to the rehab department, where she was told they had only an outpatient program.

Frustrated, she called PMCH and talked to a social worker assigned to the pediatric rehab unit, who answered all her questions about the program and the facility. Bootsie was very impressed by their program and quite relieved to know one was available. After weighing the options, she thought PMCH was the best choice for Benjamin.

We both found it hard to believe BHC didn't have a pediatric rehab program, and we decided that I would try to get more information. As a pastor, I've had contact with the chaplaincy departments at various hospitals. I've learned when I follow a patient or family through a particular roadblock in a hospital, a chaplain is often a good resource to resolve the problem or to refer me to the proper place.

I decided to call the Spiritual Care Department at BHC. Because BHC was a part of a network of hospitals, when I asked to speak to a chaplain, they connected me with a chaplain that cared for all the hospitals in the group. When I explained our situation and my wife's experience earlier in the day, he said, "I know there is a pediatric rehab unit, because it's one of the units where I'm assigned." He went on to explain that it was housed at one of the other hospitals in the group, not BHC. He said I needed to talk to a woman named Charlie, and he gave me her direct number.

In the early afternoon, Bootsie called Charlie and left a message. The call was returned at about five. Charlie said, "I'm not the person you need to talk to, but that person has gone home for the day."

Wow. Talk about frustrating! The moral of this story: when dealing with an extended physical illness of a loved one, the emotional toll can be huge. Persistence pays off, and sometimes circumstances play a role. Since my wife was so impressed with her contact at PMCH and so frustrated with contacts in the other hospital network, she chose to take BHC off the list of possibilities.

On Wednesday evening, Dr. Padgett again talked to Bootsie about a rehab unit. There was a possibility the rehab unit at Home Hospital, where Benjamin was currently, might create a space. The Home Hospital Rehab Unit was an adult one with a high percentage of people recovering from a stroke or joint replacement. Being closer to home would be terrific, but we thought it best for Benjamin to be in a unit focusing on pediatric patients. She told Dr. Padgett we'd prefer PMCH, if it was possible.

Each day, Benjamin improved physically. On Thursday, it was easier for him to go to the bathroom if I carried him, but with assistance, he could use his walker to get there. More good news came from Dr. Nuckols: when he did his typical neurological examination on Thursday, he dismissed our son into the pediatrician's care. He knew about the plan to go to a pediatric rehab unit and agreed. He said Dr. Padgett could help us with those details. As a precaution, Dr. Nuckols wanted to continue to do one IVIG treatment a week for the next four weeks to make sure Benjamin was through the acute stage of the GBS. We welcomed this news enthusiastically, and we hoped the worst was behind us.

The social worker gathered the needed information for the transfer to PMCH. Physical and occupational therapy had to evaluate Benjamin to see if he qualified for the program in Indianapolis. Since Dr. Nuckols had released him, we hoped the transfer would happen on Friday.

In the midst of all the activity on Thursday afternoon, the pediatric administrator came to say Benjamin no longer had any visitor restrictions. Restrictions weren't lifted for the hospital, but the doctors and nursing professionals recognized Benjamin's need for interaction with his peers and had been working several days to make that happen. Under-aged visitors would come up a back stairway to avoid being seen by too many people. I don't know who made that decision, but there was no way we would question it.

Benjamin, of course, was thrilled. Immediately, he started texting for friends to come. We expected to move him to PMCH on Friday, so it was only a small window of opportunity, but something was better than nothing. Almost anything out of the ordinary, anything different from usual routine in the hospital, was a welcomed diversion. Even on short notice, Benjamin had a couple of friends visit on Thursday evening, a big boost to his morale.

But Thursday night was a long and emotional night. Not long after going to bed, Benjamin began crying. He wasn't happy with the move to a different hospital. Change has always been difficult for him, and the routine at Home Hospital had become familiar and comfortable. Up until then, the primary focus had been on treating his medical needs. Physical therapy was minimal. The move to PMCH was for therapy—a definite change of focus. I'm sure our young son had some fears of how hard physical therapy might push him. Therapy hurt.

In addition to being afraid of what was coming at the new hospital, he was also grieving all the things he was missing. Saturday was the Monticello Christmas parade, and Benjamin was supposed to march in front of the high school band as one of the two carriers of their banner. He was also missing all the traditional church activities leading up to Christmas. He'd also have to skip a middle school trip to a special Christmas program in Indianapolis. The family tradition of attending the Purdue Christmas Show was just over a week away. We were also scheduled as a family to travel to Israel after the first of the year, and it had become apparent the trip would need to be delayed.

Bootsie told me she crawled into bed with Benjamin to comfort him. He eventually went to sleep, but how could she sleep? She was hanging on the edge of his mattress, processing his fears, and of course, blanketed in her own worry.

I arrived early on Friday morning so she could get away from the hospital for two or three hours. We expected the move to Indianapolis in the afternoon, and she hadn't been home since Sunday. She went home to repack, to get a break from the hospital, and to regroup a bit.

Wouldn't you know it? While Bootsie was home, the social worker came to say PMCH wanted to wait until Monday to make the transfer. We'd be spending the weekend at Home Hospital.

I called my wife to let her know of the change of plans. She'd just gotten in the car after packing for the new hospital and was headed back to Lafayette. By then, she was barely holding on emotionally. My phone call was all she needed to push her over the edge. When we hung up, she told me later, she just started crying. She couldn't hold it together any longer. Through tears, she turned the car around and went home, not wanting to carry the suitcase packed for Indianapolis into the Lafayette hospital.

When she got home, she couldn't stop crying. This was one of her lowest points in the journey to date. She just sat in the family room, sobbing. In the midst of her tears, she prayed, "God, I just need someone to give me a big hug right now."

As she finished her prayer, the doorbell rang. She didn't want to answer it. The doorbell rang again. She didn't know who was there, but she felt a strong impetus to answer.

It was Angie, a member of the church, whom my wife didn't know very well. Angie's husband had recently recovered from a long hospitalization and rehab. She could tell Bootsie had been crying.

Without saying a word, Angie gave her a big hug. She understood what Bootsie was going through. It was as if she was sent directly as God's answer to Bootsie's prayer.

When we couldn't make the transition to PMCH on Friday, it was a real disappointment. We'd been making contacts, working to get this to happen for several days. Benjamin's IVIG treatments were over. We just wanted to get on with the next step in his recovery. But it wasn't to be.

As disappointed as we were, this turn of events became a hidden blessing from God. Since visitation restrictions were lifted for him, Benjamin now had the weekend to welcome guests. On Friday night, a group of seven people from the church came to play games. They brought Balderdash with them, which was a good game for ten of us to play. We laughed a lot. Benjamin remembers the evening fondly. "It was nights like that that kept me going through all of it."

On Saturday, there was a steady flow of visitors. The hospital room was so crowded at one point that we moved to the playroom at the end of the pediatric hallway for more room and more chairs. Fortunately, there were no other patients on our end of the floor, so the nurses could be accommodating.

Of course Benjamin appreciated adult visitors, but as a normal boy, he had longed for company closer to his own age. Those extra three days in Lafayette with young visitors were good for his spirits. The transition to the Indianapolis hospital was now easier to face. I'm not sure we absorbed the lesson at the time, but after the fact, it was easy to see that Benjamin needed this time of being social before the move to Indianapolis.

As caregivers, we had a delicate balancing act. On the one hand, we needed to be advocates for Benjamin. But on the other, when things didn't work out as we would have liked, patience was required—sometimes a lot of it. Perhaps God had another plan, maybe even a more perfect plan, in mind.

Chapter 7

Special Visitor

Dr. Padgett made his rounds on Monday morning at about eight, and he discharged Benjamin from Home Hospital. He encouraged us to get to the Indianapolis hospital quickly to get the rehabilitation therapy started.

At about eleven thirty, we pulled up to the front door of the new hospital. My first memory of this hospital is the never-ending prerecorded message as we got Benjamin out of the car. It warned people about the H1N1 virus and asked that we take precautions if we had flu-like symptoms. The message also spoke of visitor restrictions because of the threat of H1N1. This was a reminder from the very beginning that there'd be little outside social contact during Benjamin's stay at this hospital.

We were instructed to go directly to his room, and the nurses started their intake procedure. The medical procedures were nothing new. His two hospitalizations in Lafayette had mainly been medical with minimal therapy, but at PMCH the main priority was physical therapy, not medical treatment. Every department that would work with Benjamin, including physical therapy, occupational therapy, nursing, dietary, a hospitalist, and a psychologist, did an initial assessment and explained what they'd be doing.

The pediatric hospitalist would follow him medically. Even though Benjamin wasn't there for medical treatment, they'd still monitor his physical condition daily. The hospitalist would also oversee the maintenance dose of IVIG that Dr. Nuckols had ordered.

A pediatric psychologist made an initial assessment. She explained that when a child has a long-term illness, it's important to monitor his or her mental and emotional health throughout the process.

As Benjamin was there primarily for physical and occupational therapy, those initial assessments were the most involved. To establish a treatment plan, they needed to assess his abilities. In Lafayette, physical therapy happened once a day for twenty to thirty minutes. The new plan at PMCH included three sessions each day of physical therapy and two sessions of occupational therapy with each session lasting forty-five minutes to an hour.

During the intake process, Benjamin asked a nurse, "Does Peyton Manning [the NFL football quarterback who the hospital was named after] ever stop by?"

The nurse said that he normally came by to see patients about once a year, but they never knew when. Because of the H1N1 concerns and visitor precautions, she was sure he wouldn't be coming any time soon. Also, the Colts were in contention for the playoffs, and they wouldn't want their quarterback to get sick.

On Tuesday, Pastor Alex, the associate pastor from the church, came to visit Benjamin, which he appreciated, and was about to leave when one of the nurses came in. A little giddy and starry-eyed, she said, "No one should go anywhere. We have a special visitor on the floor to see you. But I can't tell you who it is."

We all just looked at one another. *Do you think it's really him? Do you think Peyton Manning is actually on the floor?*

Even though Pastor Alex was ready to leave, we invited him to stay and check out the visitor. Sure enough, in about fifteen minutes, Manning came walking into Benjamin's room. He called Benjamin by name and gave him some gifts with the Colts logo. Benjamin was thrilled. A member of the public relations office of the hospital traveling with Manning said he wouldn't sign any autographs, but we could get our picture taken with him.

Wow! What an unexpected surprise! To think he visits the hospital only once a year, and we just happened to be there on the day he came. Benjamin's main concern was physical therapy, but meeting Peyton Manning was certainly a special bonus.

Benjamin had an outside visitor of some sort every day. Because it was December and just a few days from Christmas, most of these visiting groups brought gifts. It may not seem like a big deal, but these visits did a lot to lift Benjamin's spirits and to make the hospital stay more bearable. Visitors included a group of airline pilots, supervised dogs, singers from the Yuletide Christmas Celebration held at the Repertory Theater in downtown Indianapolis (this was the program he'd had a ticket to attend with his school group). And, of course, Santa Claus came to visit. All were appreciated, but none of them, including Santa Claus, was as memorable as Peyton Manning coming to his hospital room.

I was in Indianapolis for most of the week. I returned home only one time, spending Thursday night in my own bed. Bootsie stayed in Benjamin's room each night while I stayed with friends who lived a few miles away. She never left the hospital except when Benjamin did. I don't know if that was the best for her or Benjamin, but her mothering nature couldn't bear the thought of him being alone at the hospital. She wanted to be there for her son. At least if she was present, she had a sense that she was doing all she could to help him recover fully. Whatever the reason, she didn't leave the hospital.

Monday was filled with orientation and assessments. On Tuesday, the real work began. Benjamin had three sessions of physical therapy spaced throughout the day. The therapists had goals, but they also aimed to make therapy fun. They worked on strength and upper-body control using a four-wheel scooter. The scooter was a platform about one-foot square with a wheel on each corner. They'd help Benjamin get on his knees on it, and then he'd hold onto a towel.

The therapist would take the other end of the towel, and they'd pull him around the hallway. This was a lot of fun.

On the first day, it was a challenge just to be pulled around the hallway. As the week progressed and he got stronger, they'd weave back and forth in the hallway and fling him around corners. He was having fun as his balance and strength improved. Toward the end of the week, they took him to an infrequently traveled hospital corridor with a ramp. This became the place he asked me to take him between scheduled therapy sessions. He enjoyed it, and it was helping him to get stronger; it was a win/win proposition.

Another memorable activity was playing the video gaming systems Wii Sports and Wii Fit. While Benjamin had fun, these activities involved movements that increased his strength and balance. He played tennis and baseball on Wii Sports, which helped his hand/eye coordination. Wii Fit involved balancing and shifting his weight from one foot to the other. It included the use of a balance board on which he stood. Benjamin really enjoyed these purposeful games. He thought they were fun, but his therapist documented them as progress.

Occupational therapy was also strategically creative. For example, in the beanbag game, Benjamin tossed a beanbag into a bucket. Afterward, he had to pick it up. They could have given him exercises to work the same muscles, but he'd have been much less motivated. This was purposeful play that got the work done.

It quickly became apparent that rehabilitation at PMCH was the right choice for Benjamin. The adult rehabilitation unit at Home Hospital didn't have all the kid-friendly and motivational techniques used in the children's hospital.

For several days, Benjamin had asked for stir-fry. I'd seen a Chinese restaurant on the way to the hospital, so I decided to get stir-fry for supper on Tuesday night. Benjamin had worked hard in therapy. It would be a good reward.

As he ate, he was so tired he must have fallen asleep, and he choked on some rice. He was very lethargic and barely responded to us. The nurse checked him and encouraged us to watch him closely because GBS could affect his swallowing. He went to sleep and slept soundly all night. He didn't have any more problems with choking, so it must have just been because of exhaustion at the end of a hard day of therapy.

One of the challenges in understanding GBS is that it can affect so many different bodily functions. Choking is a good example. Did he choke because the GBS was affecting the nerves that helped him swallow? Or was he just tired?

Lack of appetite was also a possible side effect. When he didn't eat, was the GBS causing him not to be hungry? Or was he being a picky eater? Or was he not eating as a way to have some control over events? When he was lightheaded, was it the GBS affecting his blood pressure? Or was he not drinking enough and therefore dehydration was causing low blood pressure?

Because it was all any of us could do—doctors, nurses, and parents—we responded to symptoms without really knowing whether the cause was GBS related or not.

Wednesday was another full day of therapy: three physical and two occupational. Occupational therapy focused on everyday tasks like brushing teeth, taking a shower, and getting dressed. This was his first morning session, and it would take him nearly an hour to get ready for the day.

The therapist added going up and down stairs to Benjamin's repertoire. There was one flight of stairs in our house, and he needed to go up and down it safely. Our stairway had a railing that went only halfway up, and his therapists stressed that it should extend all the way to the top. I contacted the church trustees responsible for caring for maintenance of the parsonage. When I asked if they'd install a hand railing before we came home, they promptly and generously took care of it.

When we first arrived at PMCH, we asked about allowing Benjamin to Skype his daily algebra class. The therapists were willing, but we had problems with the hospital Wi-Fi system. The

IT department of the hospital got involved and provided Benjamin with an external data modem for his laptop. Wednesday was the first day since leaving Lafayette that he'd join his algebra class on the Internet.

He was excited about connecting with his class again, but I don't think his excitement had anything to do with an appetite for learning. This Skype class was his only connection with his peers. Mr. Casey also allowed students to bring lunch back to his classroom so Benjamin could continue interacting with friends during lunchtime. Starving for peer interaction, Benjamin looked forward to lunchtime every day.

Benjamin made good progress in his therapy, but he still had a long way to go. He'd run the One America 500 Festival Mini-Marathon (13.1 miles) in May 2009, and he already had his ticket to run again in May 2010. When therapists talked about goals, Benjamin talked about running the mini-marathon that May.

At that point, he struggled to get around with his walker, so he was a long, long way from running. It seemed unrealistic that he would run in the 2010 mini-marathon. Yet having a goal could be a great motivator.

Personally, I was so out of shape, I couldn't even run a quarter mile. I toyed with the idea of talking with Benjamin about training together for the 2010 mini-marathon. He was so weak and I was so out of shape, I thought we may be on a level playing field. I knew motivation would be difficult when we returned home, and I thought training together would be a good incentive for him. After weighing the options long and hard, I wasn't sure I was up for the challenge.

I thought and thought about asking Benjamin if we could train together, but I never told anyone what I was thinking, because I didn't know if I could do it. I wasn't even sure I had enough self-discipline.

On Thursday, Benjamin continued to show progress. He was working hard and responding well to the therapists. They attempted to have him progress from his walker to a cane, but the cane didn't give him enough support. The doctor ordered a wheelchair for when he returned home. Benjamin wouldn't be confined to the wheelchair, but when we went places that involved distances, he'd need the extra assistance. And when he returned to school, it would be a must.

The neurologist in Lafayette had ordered a maintenance dose of IVIG once a week for the next month. This was the day for that treatment, so his daily routine was somewhat interrupted. Once the IVIG started running, all he could do was to sit on his bed or in a chair. The IVIG was running before algebra class, which was convenient, and the afternoon became a good time for the pediatric psychologist to check in. This was a busy time, yet it was also somewhat quiet.

Saturday was the Purdue Music Organization's Christmas Show at Purdue University. We had tickets for the performance. The Christmas Show has over three hundred college students performing. They also have a kids' choir of about fifteen to twenty children, of which Benjamin had been a member for the past two years. Attendance was a family tradition, and he really wanted to see it.

Benjamin longed for normalcy in his life. Therapy was going well, but he wouldn't be out of the hospital by Saturday. Saturday would involve fewer therapy sessions, so we asked the therapist about a field trip away from the hospital that afternoon. We didn't know if this would be allowed. And we certainly didn't want to do anything to compromise insurance eligibility.

Because he was getting close to his hospital discharge, the therapists thought it would be a good test to see how ready he was to be released. When the therapist checked with insurance, they approved the field trip.

Friday was another good day. It was amazing to see the progress. Milestones included standing for one minute without assistance and walking two flights of stairs. Benjamin required significant help with the stairs, but making that goal was progress to celebrate. Saturday included two sessions of occupational therapy and two of physical therapy. Then Benjamin received a pass to leave the hospital for the field trip.

Arriving at the Elliott Hall of Music at Purdue University, I pulled up to a handicapped entrance. We got Benjamin out of the car and into his wheelchair, and then I parked the car. I returned to Bootsie and Benjamin in his wheelchair, and we had to figure out how to get to our seats. Benjamin could sit in a normal seat, but navigating through the crowd would be problematic.

Since our seats were in the center section, maneuvering his wheelchair would be difficult, so I simply picked him up and carried him to his seat.

Each year at the Christmas Show, during the first half of the performance, they tell the Christmas story in a way that culminates with the appearance of Santa Claus. On this particular year, the story was told through the eyes of a little girl who was sick and in the hospital on Christmas. This story was all too real for us.

After the Christmas show, I returned Bootsie and Benjamin to the hospital. I wasn't overjoyed about leaving my family, but I had to drive ninety minutes back to Monticello so I could take part in the regular Sunday worship services.

Activity in the hospital was limited on Sundays. This meant a long day for my wife and son. A Colts party on the hospital floor and watching the game brought a little excitement in the afternoon. The NFL team was about to secure its place in the playoffs, so there was a lot of Colts hysteria in the area. A TV crew showed up and filmed their party.

Benjamin knew he'd be released on Monday after a full day of therapy. Change has always been hard for him, and this was no exception. As each hospital stay neared the end, his anxiety increased. This was another horrible night as he cried himself to sleep.

There were too many unknowns with this disease. He was also lamenting all the things he was missing during that season of the year. He was again asking the ever-present question "Why me?" In the face of a spiritual crisis, we don't always get an answer to the question "Why?" Often we don't get an answer to the question on this side of eternity, but I don't believe there is anything wrong with asking the question. On the cross, even Jesus cried out, "My God, My God, why have you forsaken me?" (Matthew 27:46).

After a full day of therapy, we left PMCH at about five. For dinner, we went through the drive-through of a fast-food restaurant. We all just wanted to get home.

When we arrived at seven, home had never looked so welcoming. It had been over two weeks since Bootsie and Benjamin had spent a night in their own beds. It was good to be home.

Chapter 8

Looking for the Silver Lining

We were starting to allow ourselves some hope that Benjamin was on the road to recovery. It was now five weeks since the initial onset of the GBS symptoms, so he was beyond the time frame normally associated with the acute stage. In the acute stage, GBS actively attacks and damages the nerves. Beyond the acute stage is recovery. He'd made great progress with therapy at PMCH. Now we just had to keep the progress going.

During our GBS journey, a number of contemporary Christian songs were sources of encouragement and strength. The group Kutless had released a new song in October 2009, "What Faith Can Do." The words of the song seemed written just for us:

Don't you give up now
The sun will soon be shining
You gotta face the clouds
To find the silver lining

My faith wasn't wavering, but there were definitely many uncertainties about the future. The lines "you gotta face the clouds/ to find the silver lining" was very personal. It felt like we'd faced the clouds—actually, more as if we were still in the clouds. Yet I was optimistic we'd find the silver lining. I just wanted it to come quickly.

There was also a fitting message for Benjamin:

> It doesn't matter what you've heard
> Impossible is not a word
> It's just a reason for someone not to try

For him, too little progress was a good reason for him not to try. He wouldn't get back to school before Christmas. No progress, therefore no reason to try. We did our best to motivate him, but it was a daily battle. There was a daily fight to get him to do any physical activity. We attempted to use the Wii to duplicate what they'd done in the hospital, but it wasn't the same. He always had an excuse. Or he'd say he'd do it in an hour. And when that hour was up, he'd give another justification to remain on the couch.

He did do some exercising, but it was much less than at PMCH. All he wanted to do was to sit on the couch. He slept a lot, watched TV, and played video games.

When it came to schoolwork, Skyping his algebra class each day was often the high point of his day. He insisted that nothing interfere with algebra class time. He was falling further and further behind in his other classes and homework. He would devise a plan for getting caught up with his homework, but the more the homework piled up, the harder it was for him to do anything. Playing catch-22, it seemed we were spiraling deeper and deeper into a bottomless pit.

Benjamin was always a picky eater, so nutrition and hydration became a growing challenge. Again, it was impossible to know whether his reduced appetite was because of the GBS. Or because he was depressed. Or because he just needed to control something.

It got to where everything was a battle: physical activity, homework, eating and drinking. Bootsie, as major caretaker, had to fight those battles 24/7. And it was driving her crazy. She knew he needed to move, she knew he needed to eat and drink, and she wanted him to pass the eighth grade. But how do you force a thirteen-year-old to do what he refuses to do?

As you read this section, you might think, *I wouldn't let my child get away with that. I would put my foot down. They need to just step up and be the parent, show him who the boss is.*

Even as I write this, it's hard to believe we were so ineffective as parents. Were we so physically and emotionally spent that we weren't thinking straight? Did teenage rebellion kick in and complicate our battle with GBS? Whatever the reason, those were the realities of our household at the time.

During that time, I developed what I called a texting twitch. It was a very stressful time for Bootsie and me. When she couldn't take any more, she'd text me as her way to vent. Just before I left the office for lunch or at the end of the day, she'd often text so I knew what I was walking into. Sometimes it was a review of what had happened since I was last home. Sometimes it was an assignment of what I would need to deal with when I arrived home.

I was just beginning to use texting as a means of communication, so when I received a text, it was almost guaranteed to be from Bootsie or Benjamin. After a while, I realized that every time I received a text, I'd have a small adrenaline surge of fear and anxiety until I knew the content of the text. Sometimes I was relieved that the text just asked me to pick up an item from the store on my way home. And when other people began sending texts, I'd be relieved when it wasn't from my wife or son. My texting twitch only increased over the next few months.

On Wednesday, after his discharge from PMCH, Benjamin was scheduled for his once-a-week IVIG treatment. He and his mother returned to the pediatric unit of Home Hospital in Lafayette, where they were familiar with the treatment and Benjamin was familiar with the staff and the unit. It wasn't intimidating; it was a reunion of sorts. He'd been gone from the unit for about a week and a half. He had many stories to tell about his time at PMCH, especially about meeting Peyton Manning in person. The IVIG took about five hours, but it was a good diversion from the routine at home.

Christmas was only nine days away. Fortunately Bootsie had all of her Christmas shopping done, so she didn't need to leave the house other than for Benjamin's physical therapy appointments or for her own sanity. She baked Christmas cookies and wrapped Christmas presents for our celebration.

We had a tradition of opening our home to the congregation at Christmastime every two years. Bootsie would make Christmas cookies and candies. Members of the congregation would come and go as they pleased on a Sunday afternoon. This was the year for our open house. Bootsie wanted to skip it, but Benjamin insisted we have it. That was easy for him to say; someone else would do all the work.

The announcement was made on rather short notice at church, and those who could stopped by. It was a snowy December afternoon. It probably wasn't the smartest idea to be out on the roads that afternoon, but many braved the weather. They knew it had been a difficult six weeks for us, and this was a way to demonstrate their support.

Social interaction with someone other than his mother and father always lifted Benjamin's spirits. He remembers that afternoon fondly.

Benjamin was getting around the house pretty well with his walker. He could stand independently for a few minutes. He came down the stairs each morning and went back up the stairs at night. The continuous handrail from the first floor to the second floor was a great help. When he left the house, we always took the wheelchair, just in case the outing involved too much walking.

He attended both worship and Sunday school on the Sunday before Christmas. It was his first time to attend a Sunday morning worship service since the beginning of November. He was excited, and he got a lot of attention. On Sunday evening, he attended the Christmas party for the youth group. Even though he couldn't participate in the games, the interaction with friends was a huge boost for him. By Sunday evening, he was exhausted and ready for bed earlier than usual.

We did whatever we could to find creative ways to motivate him into physical activity. He saw them as fun outings, which they were, but as parents, we saw them as ways to get him moving.

During his last hospitalization, Benjamin had missed going with a group from his school to see the Yuletide Christmas Celebration. Performers from the show had come to visit patients on his floor at PMCH. When they heard Benjamin had missed the show, they offered our family tickets to another performance. On the Tuesday before Christmas, December 22, we went to the 11:00 a.m. show. It was enjoyable even though it involved quite a bit of physical exertion on Benjamin's part.

I felt good about the outing. But as we arrived home, he began to complain about tingling in his legs. Had he overdone it? If the feeling were from overexertion, it would pass with some rest. If GBS symptoms were returning, the exertion wouldn't have triggered the recurrence. This rare disease was so new and confusing to all of us, how were we supposed to know what to do?

After taking a nap, the tingling remained, so Bootsie called his pediatrician. Benjamin was already scheduled to go to the hospital the next day for his third maintenance dose of IVIG, so Dr. Padgett said to bring him in a few hours early for the treatment.

Once again, we went directly to the pediatric unit at Home Hospital. Dr. Padgett met us there about eight that evening, and at around eleven, Benjamin's IVIG treatment began.

On Wednesday, both Dr. Padgett and Dr. Nuckols came to see him. It was just two days before Christmas. Of course, we didn't want to do anything to compromise his health, but neither did we want him in the hospital over Christmas. Not if we could help it. The doctors had the same concern. They wanted him home for Christmas but didn't want to do any harm by discharging him.

Dr. Nuckols spent quite a bit of time examining Benjamin and then talked with Bootsie about options. Since Christmas was only two days away, he decided to give Benjamin one more IVIG treatment and then send him home. He was hopeful the treatment would get Benjamin through Christmas. But he wasn't optimistic that GBS was behind us.

As we struggled with the situation, Dr. Nuckols didn't want to overwhelm us with more bad news. He mentioned a change in treatment after Christmas, but not a different diagnosis.

In Benjamin's chart, Dr. Nuckols changed his diagnosis from GBS to chronic inflammatory demyelinating polyneuropathy (CIDP). He wrote that if Benjamin didn't respond in four weeks, he needed to begin taking an oral steroid. In its acute form, GBS normally progresses over three or four weeks. Then the disease plateaus and improves over many months. It's rare for someone with GBS to have a relapse. The chronic form, CIDP, has presenting symptoms for over eight weeks. Those with CIDP require ongoing treatments. The onset of GBS is usually preceded by a viral illness, infection, or immunization. The onset of CIDP, however, normally doesn't have a known trigger.

Benjamin was released from the hospital on the evening of December 23. He'd be spending Christmas at home.

Being home for Christmas was a relief, even though there was so much to do. Bootsie was getting things ready for our family Christmas, and I had final preparations for three Christmas Eve services on December 24.

Chapter 9

The New Normal?

On Christmas Eve, Benjamin attended the first service, which was at seven. This service was very difficult for him. He was still dealing with all the emotions and anxieties about GBS, and his greatest frustration was that he couldn't take part in the Christmas Eve service. For the last ten years, since he was three years old, he had sung a solo in that service. Understandably, he was quite disappointed he couldn't sing in the service that night.

We brought him in his wheelchair. Bootsie and my mother were also present for the seven o'clock service. They wanted Benjamin to sit with them, but he refused and was insistent that he sit alone. It was his way of dealing with the disappointment of that evening and the pain of the previous few weeks.

We had a family tradition of getting our picture taken in the front of the church sanctuary each Christmas. On this Christmas Eve, we had our picture taken in front of the sanctuary Christmas tree—with Benjamin sitting in his wheelchair. As I looked at that picture, I couldn't help but wonder if this was what future family pictures would look like—our son in a wheelchair.

After the service, church friends took Benjamin home to play games. Bootsie and my mother stayed for the second service, but not the third. Between services, many people asked Bootsie how

Benjamin was doing and how we were doing as a family. Most had genuine concern, but it was hard for them to know what to say. And trust me; they really didn't want to hear about everything we were experiencing. We were good at giving short answers and putting up a strong front, even if we were in knots on the inside.

One empathetic person began to talk to Bootsie. As they talked, the woman's eyes began to fill with tears. As she teared up, Bootsie's own tears began to run down her cheeks. The genuine compassion she experienced in that moment was comforting.

As a most welcomed respite, we enjoyed an uneventful Christmas Day. We gave Benjamin a Wii Fit balance board for Christmas (ulterior motive quite clear) and also gave him one of the Wii Fit games he'd most enjoyed at PMCH.

Whenever possible, we continued to seek ways to motivate him, to keep him active, and to rebuild his strength. On Monday, we joined the local fitness center. A fitness center and a pool could be a good source of exercise. In the pool, his legs wouldn't have to hold his full weight, and yet they'd be moving and gaining strength.

We got in the pool that night, taking a therapy ball to throw between us. This was a good outing. As parents, we were pleased with his level of activity. He was so tired when we got home, I carried him upstairs to bed.

On Tuesday, Benjamin had a follow-up appointment with Dr. Padgett. At this appointment, the doctor started talking about CIDP. Until now, the doctors had only referred to this chronic form of GBS because not enough time had passed to diagnose his illness as CIDP. Now, after nearly two months, they were ready to call it chronic.

Dr. Padgett talked about putting Benjamin on a type of chemotherapy effective in treating CIDP. As he talked with both Benjamin and Bootsie, he explained that the medicine had many side effects. Sterility was a great concern, but it didn't faze Benjamin; I don't think he even knew what it meant. All he wanted to know was whether the chemo would make him lose his hair.

On Wednesday, Benjamin walked slower and needed more help than usual getting in and out of the shower. He went to therapy but was having greater difficulty walking. His mother called the doctor's office and was advised that as long as he could stand, we could care for him at home. If he got worse and couldn't stand, we should bring him back to the hospital.

As the afternoon progressed, Benjamin got weaker and weaker. By the time I got home from work, he couldn't stand up. Bootsie called the doctor's office and was instructed to bring him back to the hospital.

We had him back in "Benjamin's suite" at the hospital by eight. The nurses did all the usual preliminaries and hooked him up to the monitors as before. As this all-too-familiar routine was unfolding, Bootsie and I struggled against an onslaught of questions. Had we pushed him too hard? Had we allowed him to do too much? We'd been pushing physical activity to rebuild his strength, and Benjamin had wanted to go places and do things to be with other people. We'd seen that as a conflict-free way to get him moving.

No matter where we turned, no one could give us definitive guidance. No one knew what to do—or what not to do. Doctors had told us more than once, "There are no statistics on a thirteen-year-old male with GBS." GBS is rare, but even rarer for a preadolescent male.

Another round of five IVIG treatments was the new plan. On Thursday, his arms began tingling again. Dr. Padgett now sounded more and more confident that our son's disease was chronic.

As a family, we were in survival mode. We were just trying to respond to the daily demands and the emotional roller coaster. Even though Benjamin's recovery was going to take a long time, I had always been hopeful he would have a full recovery. It was during this hospitalization that Bootsie confessed her fears to me: "Our little boy may never run again."

I didn't want to think about it. I didn't want to accept the possibility that our lives might be forever changed. I didn't want to consider what life would be like for our son if he was permanently disabled. Would he ever be able to live independently? Would we need to care for him the rest of his life? Even though I didn't want to think about our situation, my wife sometimes verbalized painful realities that I wanted either to ignore or to deny.

This wasn't how life was supposed to work. However, we don't always have control over how things work out. As I contemplated what the "new normal" might be like for our family, I struggled with the changes that seemed to lie ahead of us. Despite my personal struggles, the Holy Spirit constantly reminded me of God's words to the apostle Paul, "My grace is sufficient" (2 Corinthians 12:9). I'd said those words so many times. And yes, I believed them. Now it seemed that my experience of the sufficiency of God's grace would be lived on a completely new level.

We'd been quite pleased with the care Benjamin received. We had confidence in his doctors and their treatment plan. However, the chemotherapy drug seemed like such a drastic step. We talked about getting a second opinion before any chemo, but we didn't want to offend Benjamin's doctors. Nevertheless, as parents, we needed to be as certain as we could before starting this seemingly extreme treatment.

We all spent New Year's Eve in the hospital. We had a family tradition of putting a jigsaw puzzle together before midnight on that holiday. I found a puzzle with dimensions that would fit on his hospital table, and we completed it before midnight. As soon as we watched the ball drop, we all went to bed. Benjamin had his bed. My wife had her bed. And rather than traveling home as usual, I slept on the cushioned bench.

On New Year's Day, Benjamin received his third treatment of IVIG. Since it was a national holiday *and* Friday, most people would have a long weekend. While this wasn't a convenient time to pursue a second opinion, we didn't think we could wait.

We had friends who lived in Rochester, Minnesota. They happened to go to the same church as the head of pediatrics at Mayo Clinic and were good friends with him. With his permission, they sent us his email address. Bootsie sent him an email with the basics of our journey. In the past, Benjamin had started improving by day four of the IVIG treatments. This time was different. He wasn't improving. The pediatrician at the Mayo Clinic confirmed that, given the facts of the case as she shared them, Benjamin's doctors were taking a reasonable course of action.

He went on to indicate that if we wanted a second opinion, they'd be willing to see Benjamin in Rochester. He also gave us the name of a doctor he knew at the Bippus Hospital for Children, which was less than two hours away. He believed BHC could meet our needs as well as the Mayo Clinic. And BHC was much closer for us.

Benjamin was angry and distressed. He was angry about having GBS. The disruption of daily life, the complications of not being in school, and the tests and treatments with all their side effects had all upset his sense of equilibrium. He was irritated with his mother for making him get the flu vaccine. And now, because of all his circumstances, he was becoming depressed, with dark clouds threatening his mental sky. His (and our) worst fears were coming true. Apparently he had CIDP. He'd be receiving treatments for the rest of his life.

After I left on Saturday evening, Benjamin had a meltdown. Bootsie later observed that the meltdowns always came when I wasn't around. Maybe that was the case. It was certainly true that it was more difficult for her to handle them by herself. She hadn't wanted to burden me with Benjamin's crisis, because she knew I was back in Monticello, finishing preparations for Sunday morning.

My wife and I talked on Sunday morning before I left for church, and she gave me an update. We agreed she'd broach the idea of a second opinion when the doctor came in on Sunday.

Meanwhile, I just wanted to get through the morning worship services so I could get to the hospital to be with my wife and son. This illness had become much more than an interruption; it had become the center of our daily lives.

Dr. Keller, a pediatrician in the same group as Dr. Padgett, was the doctor making rounds on Sunday. When Bootsie talked with him about a second opinion, he had no objection and went to the nurse's station to make some phone calls. When he came back, he told Bootsie that when Benjamin's IVIG treatment was finished at about four that afternoon, he'd be discharged. We could then immediately take Benjamin to BHC for a second opinion.

It was about 10:45 a.m. Bootsie knew the second worship service had begun at ten thirty. She felt it was vital that I know about these new plans, and she wanted me to tell the congregation so they might pray.

She called the church during the service. An usher answered the phone and wrote her message on a piece of paper. When the ushers came forward for the offering and the choir was singing the offertory anthem, an usher handed me the note. It simply said, "Benjamin will be transferred to BHC this afternoon for a second opinion." Obviously, I'd known things would happen after we'd talked about getting a second opinion. Still, I was surprised we'd made the transition to BHC so quickly.

It isn't typical for an usher to hand me a note during a service. Even though he did it discretely, people saw him do it. A note handed to the pastor during a service normally means the message is very important; otherwise, it could wait until after the service. So those who saw the note being handed to me naturally thought, *What is wrong?*

After the offering, I told the congregation Benjamin would be transferred to BHC later that day. I asked the members of our congregation to pray for us, to pray that Benjamin not have chronic GBS, and to pray for healing. We also wanted prayer for a definite diagnosis as well as for wisdom to know what to do next.

At the end of the worship service, the associate pastor led in prayer for Benjamin and our family. The congregation gathered around me as I knelt at the altar, and Pastor Alex prayed.

Over the previous two months, we'd done our best to keep the congregation and prayer chain updated on Benjamin's condition. I'd mentioned updates from the pulpit when there was new information to share. I tried to strike a balance between keeping them informed while trying not to dwell on our situation too much. On that morning, there was a genuine outpouring of concern and prayer by the congregation directed heavenward for us. I knew they cared. That moment was hugely affirming and encouraging. It was a time when I felt sustained by the prayers of the congregation. I wished Bootsie and Benjamin had been with me to share in the moment.

After the service, the chairperson of the Staff Parish Committee (the personnel team in the church) told me to take a couple of weeks off to be with my family. This was an especially kind gesture. Even though I'd been staying connected with the church during Benjamin's hospitalizations, it was quite a relief to know I didn't have to worry about my balancing act while Benjamin was in the hospital again. Even though I believe I was managing my responsibilities appropriately, the church leadership recognized that my full attention needed to be with my family—something I might not have recognized on my own.

Bootsie had called for help from a member of the church who normally attends the first service. She needed this friend to sit with Benjamin while she returned to Monticello to pack for the transfer to BHC. She arrived home about the same time I got back from church. Since she didn't know how long we'd be away from home or whether she could stay in the room, for the greatest flexibility she packed a separate suitcase for each of us.

When we returned to the hospital, Benjamin's IVIG treatment was nearly finished. We just had to complete the discharge papers and then drive to the Bippus Hospital for Children, where he would be admitted.

The couple from the church graciously offered to transport Benjamin. This arrangement allowed Bootsie and me to follow in our car and talk. So much had happened since our morning conversation, and we didn't know what was next. Driving together without Benjamin present gave us time to talk and to figure out a plan for moving forward together with this new development.

Chapter 10

Second Opinion

At the time, all admissions to BHC passed through the emergency room. Even though the doctor in Lafayette had made all the arrangements, it felt like we were being admitted for the first time. As we all pulled up to the ER entrance at about 6:00 p.m., we got a wheelchair for Benjamin and took him into the hospital. Our church friends headed back to Monticello. Their warm act of kindness was such a help for us.

God often reminded us to receive graciously the kindness offered by others. His grace was often extended to us through the hands and feet of those with whom we came in contact day by day.

Many people, throughout our journey with GBS, reached out with acts of kindness and encouragement. Though we tried to say thank you to all, God notices every act of grace and kindness done out of Christian love and compassion. In Matthew 25, Jesus said that whenever you perform an act of kindness and compassion to another person, especially a person who isn't able to do anything in return, it's as if you have done the act for him.

We were later told that a group of people also met in the church sanctuary on Sunday evening to pray for Benjamin. We will never be able to thank everyone adequately who remembered us in prayer throughout this long journey.

After leaving Bootsie with Benjamin in the ER waiting room, I parked the car. By the time I returned to the ER, Benjamin and Bootsie were in an examination room, beginning the admission process. This admission process was very different from those at Home Hospital or PMCH. Even though they expected us, we'd arrived one hour before the shift change. We did a lot of waiting, but finally, around 10:00 p.m., Benjamin arrived in his room. By the time he got to his room, he was an emotional wreck. His underlying anger about being sick was compounded by fears about this new, unfamiliar hospital. Would they find something new, or would they confirm his diagnosis? Naturally, Benjamin's attitude affected his mother, who wasn't in the best frame of mind either. My role as buffer and encourager resumed.

It was very late in the day. We were all physically and emotionally exhausted as he got settled enough to go to bed. Enough was enough; he insisted his mother not stay with him. I agreed they needed time away from one another.

At almost midnight, Bootsie and I arrived at a hotel about a mile away that was affiliated with the hospital. It was nothing fancy. The blinds didn't close, but we were on the twelfth floor. As we glanced out our window, we saw that ours was the tallest building, so no one would be looking in our window. We were exhausted, and all we wanted to do was lay our heads on the inviting pillows. We'd be back at BHC in six or seven hours.

We returned to BHC by seven so we'd be in the room when the neurologist made morning rounds. When the neurologist arrived at about nine with copies of Benjamin's charts from his previous admissions, he wanted to repeat two of the tests from November (MRI and EMG). Additionally, he wanted a spinal tap. The MRI would rule out spine or hip problems that might have been missed in the previous MRI. The other two tests would indicate whether the GBS was still actively attacking his body. After eight weeks, if his autoimmune system was fighting against itself, that would confirm the CIDP diagnosis.

In addition to the diagnostic testing, Benjamin had daily physical therapy. He didn't like the therapy because it pushed him out of his comfort zone. He'd grown comfortable using his walker as support over the last two months. Now they wanted him to walk without it. He could do this hard work, but he wasn't very motivated; he simply didn't want to do it. The therapist's persistence won out, but Benjamin wasn't too pleased. It was a lot to ask of anyone, but especially a thirteen-year-old. The MRI was done on Monday, the EMG on Tuesday, and the spinal tap on Wednesday.

Visitors were strictly limited at BHC. We used a code when coming or going from the locked unit. Since Benjamin was there only for testing and therapy, we were permitted to take him off the floor where his room was located and meet visitors in the library.

On Tuesday, we were glad to welcome two visitors from his school: the assistant principal, Mr. Provo, and Benjamin's guidance counselor, Mrs. Deno. They'd called to say they were coming, so we were prepared to have Benjamin in the library to meet them. They were concerned for Benjamin's health, but also came to talk about his academic progress. He still hadn't completed all his assignments from the first semester. And with a hospitalization at the beginning of his second semester, keeping up would be difficult. Although he didn't talk about it, Benjamin worried whether he'd need to take eighth grade over again. His mother and I had the same concerns.

Mr. Provo and Mrs. Deno were sympathetic to his situation and needs. They proposed he just forget about unfinished work from the first semester. Teachers had already turned their grades in. English and algebra would be his only requirements in the second semester. As he improved and returned to school, he'd rejoin his other classes, but wouldn't be required to turn in missed work. Benjamin would start fresh from that point forward.

This plan lifted a huge weight. Benjamin had felt more and more overwhelmed as he fell behind in his schoolwork. As parents, we were also relieved. A major stress, strife, and bone of contention was now removed.

On Wednesday afternoon, the doctor talked with us about the test results. The MRI looked normal. There was nothing with the EMG or spinal tap to indicate GBS was active in Benjamin's system. This information was such a relief and clearly an answer to prayer. Our prayer that he not have the chronic form of GBS was also answered. It was also our prayer that we'd have a definitive diagnosis. We'd received a definitive diagnosis, but there were still a lot of questions. Why was Benjamin so weak? Why did he continue to have the tingling sensations and weakness that took us back to the hospital?

Even though the acute stage of the GBS had passed, he was still healing. Initially we were told that full recovery would take many months. Of course Benjamin's weakness was compounded by his being in bed and inactive for most of the last two months. One doctor told us that, as a rule of thumb, it takes three days to regain the strength lost for each day in a hospital bed. Benjamin had been in a hospital bed for twenty-three of the previous sixty days. In addition to strength lost by being in bed, he also had a disorder that made him weak. Weakness was to be expected, but with perseverance and hard work, he'd regain his strength.

After the report from the neurologist, a psychologist met with us. She first talked with Bootsie and me. Then she talked with Benjamin in our presence. With the following story, she explained what was going on:

A few years ago I went to a restaurant and ordered a burrito. I loved Mexican food, and I loved burritos. A couple hours after eating the burrito, I got very sick. I started vomiting, and I felt as sick as I've ever felt. I just wanted to die. It was determined I had gotten food poisoning from the burrito I ate. In a few days, everything was back to normal.

Then something unexpected happened. I went out to eat one day with friends, and I ordered a burrito. This burrito was just fine, but after eating it, my body remembered what happened the last time I ate a burrito and responded in a similar way. I didn't have food poisoning, but I felt like I was going to throw up.

She went on to explain that whenever Benjamin's body had pain or feelings like those he'd had when the acute GBS attacked his body, the intense fear of a relapse caused his body to respond in a similar way. The fear was real. The body's response was real. Benjamin wasn't faking it or imagining it. Nevertheless, medically, Benjamin's symptoms weren't a physical relapse of GBS.

The psychologist recommended Benjamin see a colleague at an outpatient clinic to learn to deal with this fear. Often, our fears, irrational or otherwise, are very real to us. These fears can affect our behavior and responses in life. Cognitively, Benjamin may have understood what the psychologist told him, but that didn't mean his response would change.

At the time, we embraced the conclusions of the BHC doctors. We had no doubt psychological factors influenced Benjamin's recovery, but these conclusions seemed so simple—even too simple to explain what we had endured in the last two months.

What we've discovered over time is that the physical ups and downs Benjamin experienced in those first two or three months after diagnosis were common. At a time when longer hospital admissions were commonplace, a GBS patient might be in the hospital for several months. During the longer hospital stay, patients would experience physical setbacks, and it would be considered a normal part of their recovery. However, in our situation, with each discharge we expected only progress. Setbacks caused us to believe that something was going wrong. We were concerned that it was a sign of relapse or the chronic form of GBS.

Another frustration for Benjamin and other GBS patients was that it felt like no one understood. He was dealing with other adolescent and emotional issues during his recovery, but he knew he was tired. He knew he didn't have the energy he'd had just three months earlier. Even though Benjamin's experience was similar to those of other GBS patients, I'm not sure the team at BHC understood the impact of the long physical recovery. Clinically, there was no evidence of active GBS in his body, so the consensus seemed to be "just put it behind you and move on."

This lack of understanding and empathy is a common experience of those recovering from GBS. It causes GBS patients to begin doubting what they are experiencing. The doubting further shakes their self-confidence, which is already fragile.

We will never know with certainty, but I believe all of Benjamin's follow-up hospitalizations after the initial diagnosis in November 2009 through January 2010 were simply responses to the normal challenges of GBS recovery. At the time, our fears caused us to focus too much on the possibility of relapse or CIDP.

Once we had the report from the BHC team of doctors, it was time to look forward. Benjamin was talking about running again, though he hadn't run since sometime in October. The mini-marathon was about four months away. He'd need to do serious training if he was going to participate in the race.

As I mentioned before, I'd been thinking of making a commitment to train with Benjamin for the 13.1-mile mini-marathon. I was in poor physical condition, and Benjamin had far to go in his rehabilitation, but I thought maybe we could motivate one another. I also knew that if he ran the race, someone needed to be with him. It made sense that I would be that someone.

I talked to Benjamin about my crazy idea. I shared with him that I wasn't sure I could do it, but I was willing to do my best. I think he was pleased not to be alone with difficult physical goals ahead of him. I was willing to make sacrifices as well. And so we planned to train together for the mini-marathon.

Discharge from the hospital was scheduled for Thursday, but a snowstorm was forecast to hit the area overnight. Local government officials expected the city to be shut down by the storm until roads could be cleared. Bootsie and I had left the hospital to sleep on the first three nights there. Because of the incoming storm, the staff said we could both stay in his room. I slept on the bench seat under his window, and his mother slept on a rollaway bed.

The storm hit as predicted. Since we lived about one hundred miles away, they told us we could spend another night before returning home. While we wanted to be home, going home wasn't worth the risk, given the condition of the roads and Benjamin's weakened state. After another night in his hospital room, we went home on Friday morning.

It had been a very different hospitalization than previous ones. We left with what we needed to know: there was no evidence that GBS (or CIDP) was actively attacking Benjamin's body. And he was walking without the assistance of a walker for the first time in nearly two months.

As we left the hospital, we were thankful for the ways we believed God used the medical team at BHC to help us on our journey. We were thankful for the prayers of our church, friends, and family. Did their prayers change Benjamin's physical condition? We will never know for sure, but we do know prayers sustained us through those days. Maybe we would see some light at the end of the tunnel.

Chapter 11

Shooting Pain

While the second opinion from BHC was a relief, it certainly didn't mean life was back to normal. Strength and stamina were still issues for Benjamin. Schoolwork went much better, but he was taking only two classes. He joined his algebra class by way of computer each day. When he felt up to it, he'd actually go to class. He met his English teacher once a week after school. Without homework piling up, we all felt less pressure.

Benjamin went to physical therapy three days a week and participated appropriately. However, at home he refused to do his daily exercises. This, of course, caused growing tension. The exercises were boring to Benjamin, and in his opinion, they were of no help, so he didn't see any reason to do them.

Every evening when we could, we played Wii Fit. It was a fun game to play when we couldn't convince him to do his assigned exercises. And it was certainly better than doing nothing. We took turns choosing which games we'd play. Bootsie and I cleverly chose games requiring him to do movements similar to the exercises he wasn't doing.

Benjamin and I went to the gym three nights a week. We'd each start on the treadmill. He'd set his treadmill at a much slower speed than I set mine, but at least he was walking. After walking ten minutes, he'd go to the weight room. My goal was to work up to jogging one mile. I started at a fast walking pace then added some jogging. Walking wasn't a problem, but the jogging was a challenge. I worked on jogging one tenth of a mile then two tenths, and so on. When I got up to a half mile, I'd take a break. I was sweating and needed to catch my breath, so I stopped to drink a bottle of water.

The mini-marathon was less than four months away. Even the thought of walking 13.1 miles was overwhelming. If I wanted to jog it, I had a long way to go, and so did Benjamin.

When he was discharged from BHC, Benjamin was referred to a psychologist in their outpatient clinic. The psychologist was to help with fear and anxiety issues. Benjamin didn't want to go, but we managed to convince him to get in the car. When we arrived for the appointment, he refused to get out of the car. I weighed our options. He was small enough that I could physically remove him from the car, but I didn't believe that approach would help the session with the psychologist. Besides, we were in a public parking garage, and we could have made quite a scene. I chose not to argue; I simply told him that he could stay in the car if he wanted, but we would take away his cell phone until he did meet with the psychologist. As his mother and I got out of the car, he chose to follow.

While the psychologist was quite insightful, two problems surfaced. First, Benjamin wasn't a willing participant. Second, the psychologist's schedule allowed him to meet with Benjamin only once a month—too infrequently to establish a trusting relationship.

At home, Benjamin became more and more depressed. He and his mother locked horns often. They argued about exercise. They argued about his eating habits. They argued about his fluid intake. Bootsie wanted him to follow the doctor's orders. Benjamin's interpretation was that she only wanted to control him. Again, there were no clear answers. Was this a naturally rebellious thirteen-year-old? Was this a household battle for control? Was the depression directly related to his recovery from GBS? Or was it a natural response to a long recovery?

Bootsie was in regular contact with the pediatrician's office. Since the middle of November, they'd monitored Benjamin's emotional condition. At an appointment in mid-January, when Dr. Padgett talked about depression, Benjamin declared he didn't want an antidepressant. The doctor said if he changed his mind, to let him know. Knowing his patient needed an antidepressant, he wanted to give Benjamin a measure of control when so much of his life felt out of his control.

Ten days later, after a terribly conflicted weekend, Benjamin asked Bootsie to call the doctor. He was ready to take medicine to help his depression. He had had an occasional Tylenol or Motrin in the last three months. He was given medications in the hospital, but this antidepressant was the first prescription we'd filled since the onset of GBS. In retrospect, I find that amazing.

On the next evening, January 28, Benjamin and I went to the gym. He tried running for the first time since October. He ran one minute. One minute may not have been a lot, but it was a start. For Benjamin, this was a milestone in his recovery. Finally, he felt good about something.

At home, he went to his usual spot on the couch. After a few minutes, he began having pain in one of his legs. He described it as an electrical shock, a shooting pain that traveled down his leg. Pain began in one leg and then the other. The shooting pain happened repeatedly, about every two to three minutes. We thought he'd overexerted himself at the gym, and we were supportive when he decided to go to bed early. Rest would help, and he'd be better in the morning, we reasoned.

In the morning, however, the shooting pain was even worse. The more time passed, the more painful his legs became. With each nerve firing, Benjamin yelled out in pain. His mother called the doctor to see what we should do. He told her to give him Motrin and to massage his legs and keep them warm.

It was Friday. With the recommended treatment, we hoped the pain would subside over the weekend. Unfortunately, there was no improvement. The pain escalated. The shooting pain was now in both legs and extended into his feet.

On Monday, Bootsie called the pediatrician's office for an appointment. Something more was needed. Watching him in pain was awful. His crying out every two to three minutes was more than emotionally wearing. After examining Benjamin, Dr. Padgett diagnosed him with neuropathy. A person might experience neuropathy for many reasons, he explained. Simply stated, neuropathy is a general description of the pain a person feels because of a dysfunction of his or her nervous system.

Neuropathy is common in GBS patients. The previous tingling in his legs and arms was also called neuropathy. What he was now experiencing was more painful. Doctors had warned us he might experience pain with GBS. We were neither expecting nor prepared for the intensity of the pain our son was suffering.

To stop the pain, Dr. Padgett prescribed a common medicine for neuropathy. He also referred Benjamin to the neurologist. The first available appointment was a week from Friday, eleven long days away.

We immediately started him on the medicine. But there was no relief. Benjamin yelled less with pain if he focused on other activities. The shooting pain didn't stop, but with his mind focused elsewhere, he didn't yell out as much. But keeping him distracted wasn't easy. We were able to succeed only for short periods.

Before the neuropathy pain, Benjamin had been sleeping eleven or more hours a night. Now he was sleeping only six. Lack of sleep created a domino effect. When he didn't get his sleep, he was more irritable during his waking hours. When he was tired, it was hard for him to experience anything other than pain. Consequently, the pain seemed to worsen.

Coping with neuropathy was certainly difficult for Benjamin. For his mother and me, the situation was physically and emotionally exhausting. I would go to work during the day, so I had a bit of a reprieve. His mother was with him all day, and she was the one he normally called out to at night.

Benjamin was getting six hours of sleep, which meant Bootsie was getting fewer. At bedtime, she'd go to his room and rub his feet and legs until he could relax. When he fell asleep, she found she still needed to quiet her mind from the stresses of the day.

When shooting pain woke Benjamin at four or five in the morning, Bootsie's night of rest was over as well. Lack of sleep was an obvious reason for her physical exhaustion. On top of that, Benjamin's constant yelling out in pain added a heavy emotional toll.

On Thursday, Bootsie called Dr. Padgett's office with an update on the neuropathy. Besides the audible screams, now coming every sixty to ninety seconds, there was a noticeable, involuntary twitch at the site of the nerve pain.

Bootsie made the call from another room, away from where Benjamin sat on the couch. As she talked to the doctor's nurse, the nurse asked, "Is that Benjamin I hear in the background?"

"Yes," Bootsie replied. "He's down the hall and in another room." From her response, it was clear the nurse felt great empathy for him and for Bootsie. The nurse said she'd talk with the doctor and call back.

When she called back, she said she had been unable to get Benjamin an earlier appointment with the neurologist. She also said that she was calling in a prescription that the pediatrician ordered for a lotion that would help the pain in his feet.

Benjamin began once again to Skype his algebra class. We muted his computer microphone so the class wouldn't hear him crying out in pain. In addition, because of his neuropathy pain, he could no longer go after school for English tutoring.

By then, Benjamin didn't have many visitors. One friend who did come over during that painful time of neuropathy later said she was "freaked out" by the way his legs twitched. Flinching from the nerve pain was so much a part of Benjamin's daily experience that he didn't even consider how his pain might affect others.

With each passing day, we were more and more desperate to find something to relieve his unrelenting pain. Monday brought no relief, and more areas of his body were affected—now it was also his arms and back. Bootsie took him back to the pediatrician.

Dr. Padgett really wanted the neurologist involved, but he knew that appointment was still four days away. He saw how much Benjamin suffered and wanted to make him more comfortable. In an attempt to relieve the pain, he added another prescription.

On Tuesday, Bootsie again called the pediatrician, reporting that now Benjamin told of nerve firings in his jaw, face, and chest. While we couldn't see the twitching in these new areas, the type of pain seemed consistent.

Wednesday brought no relief, and the affected areas were getting worse. Bootsie again called Dr. Padgett's office. Nothing really had changed except the neuropathy was getting worse. The doctor added yet another prescription for nerve pain, this time prescribing a narcotic for severe pain. We hoped and prayed these medications would bring relief.

The tense atmosphere in our home was hard to describe. For about two weeks, our child was in ever-increasing pain. As parents, we wanted to get his pain relieved. At the same time, we were simply unable to do anything that helped. Benjamin was already dealing with depression. Now constant nerve pain and sleeplessness were added into the mix. His emotional downward spiral was accelerating. Benjamin's needs were our primary concern, but Bootsie and I felt as though we were walking on eggshells.

We were at the three-month point since the onset of the GBS symptoms, and the neuropathy had been happening for only two weeks. We'd all been on this journey together, but Bootsie had been with Benjamin virtually nonstop for nearly three months. Emotionally she was on thin ice before the neuropathy, and now with greater sleep deprivation, she had to listen to her child yell in pain forty to sixty times every hour. How much worse could things possibly get? How much more could we take? I ached for both of them.

Bootsie called the pediatrician's office once again on Thursday to see if Dr. Padgett could see Benjamin again. Benjamin was being tortured with constant pain. We simply had to find a way to relieve it. As parents, we were so overwhelmed, it was hard to think straight.

Dr. Padgett was off on Thursday, so he couldn't see Benjamin. His nurse did call the neurologist's office and got Benjamin's Friday afternoon appointment moved to the morning. It wasn't a lot, but we appreciated seeing the neurologist even a few hours earlier. The pediatrician's office also said that if Benjamin got worse, we should take him to the ER.

By the time I got home in the late afternoon, Bootsie was at the end of her rope. It had been a horrible day. Benjamin's pain had intensified even further. He was tired, so his tolerance for pain was lower. We had an appointment with the neurologist in fewer than twenty-four hours, but the pediatrician's office had told us to go to the ER if he got any worse. Our journey with GBS was filled with so many unpredictable twists and turns. Should we be concerned enough to take action? Or should we hold tight and be patient?

Only hours away from seeing the neurologist, Benjamin was getting worse. We were emotionally spent and struggling to think straight. What should we do?

We decided to err on the side of caution: we'd go to the emergency room. We were immediately presented with another decision: should we go to Home Hospital in Lafayette or to BHC? We knew Dr. Nuckols was off duty. If we went to Lafayette, Benjamin probably wouldn't be seen by a neurologist. And if a different neurologist saw him, that neurologist wouldn't be familiar with his case. Benjamin had been a patient at BHC in January. Even without the same neurologist, there'd be recent records of his case. We decided to go to BHC.

When we arrived at BHC, the emergency room doctor contacted the neurologist on call. She was young and seemed to be the on-call neurology resident. After doing an examination, she said Benjamin was in no immediate danger. She didn't seem to have much empathy for our journey over the last two weeks, but it was a relief to know nothing was life threatening.

She left the room to review his chart from his January admission to BHC. After about fifteen minutes, I left the exam room where the three of us were waiting, to use the restroom. As I passed the nurses' station, I overheard the neurologist talking about Benjamin's case. She was laughing as she described his movements and his yelling out in pain. She seemed to minimize and even ridicule what she'd been told and what she'd observed in her examination.

As I continued walking to the restroom, I could feel my blood pressure rise. I wondered how I should respond? Should I confront the doctor for her lack of professionalism and blatant violation of HIPAA guidelines? I was so angry, I concluded it was wise not to confront the situation at that moment. I realized Benjamin was just another case for her. Yet a medical professional minimizing and laughing about our experience was highly offensive and hurtful.

Maybe we had needed an objective and detached evaluation, and this neurologist was certainly detached. She didn't have much insight into solving the mystery of why Benjamin had this increasing pain. Her recommendation: Keep our appointment with the neurologist in Lafayette, who regularly cares for Benjamin. Allow him to treat the condition.

As frustrating as the ER visit was, we received the welcome information that Benjamin wasn't in immediate danger. In retrospect, we probably overreacted. We could've just waited until his long-anticipated appointment with Dr. Nuckols the next day. But what if Benjamin was getting worse? Erring on the side of caution was better for us than regret if we hadn't responded and should have.

On Friday morning, we both went to Benjamin's ten thirty appointment with Dr. Nuckols. We desperately wanted—needed— answers and relief. I was fascinated by Dr. Nuckols's examination and his detailed questions. He asked Benjamin to describe the pain. Benjamin said the pain in his feet and legs was a constant burning sensation. He also had shooting pain in his legs that felt like electrical shocks.

Dr. Nuckols asked, "Where did the pain start? In which direction did the pain travel? Did it move up or down your leg?" For each leg, each arm, his back, his chest, and his face, he asked the same kind of questions.

When he finished the exam, he confirmed the pain to be consistent with damaged peripheral nerves. No surprise there. I asked Dr. Nuckols about the significance of the pain moving up or down his legs. He explained that different medications were more effective, depending on which direction the pain moved. I was intrigued by the examination and the insightfulness of his conclusions.

The doctor agreed with the prescriptions given by Dr. Padgett, although he increased some of the dosages. Benjamin was now on one antidepressant, four prescriptions for neuropathy, two narcotics for pain, lotion for his feet, vitamin B, and a pill for his upset stomach, undoubtedly caused by all the medicine he was taking.

Dr. Nuckols understood and empathized with Benjamin's pain. Dr. Padgett had started with a very conservative and measured approach to alleviating his pain. Now, after two weeks, Dr. Nuckols responded much more aggressively. He also encouraged Benjamin to move as much as possible, because he believed using his muscles would help to reduce the nerve firings that happened as he simply sat on the couch.

The next morning, Dr. Nuckols's office called to follow up on Benjamin's condition. This had never happened after other appointments. The call was even on Saturday, when his office was closed. I assumed the call had a twofold purpose: to see if Benjamin's pain was any better and to see how he was responding to all the medications.

Bootsie responded that Benjamin was much better, compared to the previous two weeks. He was like a new kid. The pain, while not completely gone, was significantly less. The atmosphere around the house was much more bearable. Things had been very tense, but now we all breathed sighs of relief.

Because of the many medications Benjamin was taking and all the possible side effects, the doctor monitored him closely. Bootsie was to call the neurologist's office every day with a report and took Benjamin to the hospital every other day for lab work and a urinalysis.

On Monday, Bootsie reported that he was much improved compared to his condition before the appointment on Friday. When the neurologist reviewed the lab results, his office called to adjust one of the medications.

On Tuesday, Benjamin had blurred vision, probably a side effect of medication. The last three days had been such a relief, but his pain was again increasing, while his appetite and activity level were decreasing. He still wasn't sleeping well, getting about six hours of sound sleep. From then on, he'd just doze off and on. He was more depressed and said he was tired of trying. Emotionally, he was a mess. He did go to school for algebra for the first time in over two weeks, the only bright spot in the day.

Bootsie worked diligently to keep all of his medications straight. She would check and double-check. She researched drug interactions to make sure something wasn't overlooked. At breakfast, she doled out thirteen pills of one sort or another, then more pills scattered throughout the day. She also had to wake Benjamin twice during the night to give him a pill. Fortunately, if he was sound asleep, she could get him to sit up and take the pill, and he'd go right back to sleep, not even remembering it in the morning.

Most nights, Bootsie still rubbed Benjamin's feet and legs when he went to bed. If he hadn't yet fallen asleep when she was done rubbing his feet and legs, he'd insist she lie down with him. After he fell asleep, she'd come to our bed between midnight and two.

On Wednesday, Bootsie called Dr. Nuckols's office with an update. She said his pain was increasing again, and he was constipated. With all the medicine he was on, constipation wasn't a surprise. She also took him to the hospital for a repeat of the lab work and a urinalysis. After the reports, the neurologist made changes and additions to Benjamin's prescriptions.

On Friday, Dr. Nuckols wanted a follow-up appointment. He was pleased with the progress, but since Benjamin still had some pain in his legs, he added one more prescription. A month prior, Benjamin hadn't been taking any prescribed medications. By the third week of February, he was on thirteen different ones.

The good news was that his physical pain had lessened. He no longer had the intense electrical, shock-type pain. The bad news was that he still needed physical therapy to renew his strength.

Benjamin just wanted to be well again. He was tired of not having energy or physical strength and stamina. He wanted to be back to school full-time. He wanted to run track. He just wanted life to be normal.

Since November, there had been signs of depression. It was situational depression; he was depressed because of the circumstances of his life, which had been interrupted and possibly changed forever by GBS. His life was out of his control, and he could do nothing about it. In late January, just before the onset of neuropathy, he'd started an antidepressant. Now his depression was worse.

Chapter 12

Emotional Nosedive

When Benjamin started the new medications, our primary goal had been to stop the intense pain. That goal was accomplished. Then we had to deal with side effects and other unwanted consequences of being on the medications. Five of his medications listed serious mental and emotional side effects, including depression, trouble concentrating, sadness, apathy, memory problems, slowed reactions, nervousness, and increased risk of suicide in youth. At least those were the side effects we were dealing with; there were others listed we hadn't yet seen.

As Benjamin later reflected on this time, he recognized that the medications caused his worsening mental instability. He was heading fast into a very, very dark place.

At home, we continued to battle over exercise, eating, hydration, and schoolwork. We tried to motivate him to do what he could do to get better. With the initial onset of GBS, we'd noticed his mental sharpness wasn't what it once was. Now, adding the side effects of the medications, it was even more difficult for him to concentrate and understand new concepts in his homework. As he was already depressed and unmotivated, the array of medications further complicated these emotions.

It was understandable that Benjamin, not seeing any improvement, had a "Why try?" attitude.

I continued to train for the mini-marathon, going to the gym three or four times a week. After the neuropathy pain was under control, Benjamin went with me a couple of those times. I was making progress, but I was still a long way from being able to conquer 13.1 miles. When I could jog a twelve-minute mile without stopping, it was a major victory for me.

Benjamin walked and later jogged on the treadmill. He was making slow progress. One night in mid-March, I was immensely relieved when he said, "Dad, I don't think I'll be able to do the mini-marathon this year. What about just doing the 5K race instead?" The One America 500 Festival had a five-kilometer (3.1 miles) race on the same day as the mini-marathon. Running a 5K race was much more realistic for both of us.

Despite our struggles, I was proud of my son's progress. Allowing him to make the decision about running only five kilometers also gave him a sense of having some control. Control was something he had lost, so it was welcomed.

During this time, I wasn't thriving, just surviving. My job, as I saw it, was to hold everything together in the church and at home. If I could do that, ignoring my own feelings and needs was easier. I had very little reserve, but I thought I was making it okay.

Then one day a leader in the church came into my office and asked if he could pray for me. As a pastor, I was accustomed to people coming to me and asking *me* to pray for *them*. It was unusual for someone to ask if he or she could pray for me. I know there were many people who prayed for our family in their personal prayer time. On this day, when the leader came into my office, I felt cared for in a way I desperately needed.

Our lives had been interrupted in so many ways. Because of Benjamin's hospitalizations in December, the church staff delayed our staff Christmas party until after the first of the year. January and February weren't very convenient either. Finally, in March, we had the party. It wasn't very Christmassy, but we had finally found time to get together for a meal.

Then, on the night of our March Christmas party, I realized how much the staff had protected me, involving me only in necessary decisions. They'd sensed the stress I was under and did what they could to lighten my load. They'd become more interdependent and team-oriented than I'd realized during those months, a good result born from the unpleasant reality of my family's situation.

At the beginning of March, Benjamin once again returned to school for his algebra class. His pain was under control as his nerves were no longer firing randomly, but he still didn't feel normal. He described his pain as a discomfort. It wasn't like anything he'd ever experienced before the "shocking" neuropathy. He compared it to the pain one feels with a burn. Initially the burn hurts intensely, but as it heals, there's lingering pain or discomfort. This residual pain or discomfort was tolerable. He was excited about returning to school, even if it was just for one hour a day.

Benjamin had been out of a normal school routine for nearly four months. He'd Skyped algebra since early December whenever possible, but he'd been physically present in the classroom only a few days before the intense neuropathy. Benjamin desperately wanted to be back in school. He wanted a full school day, but his strength and endurance simply weren't up to it. On March 15, he began attending English as well as algebra. His mother took him to school for English, then picked him up fifty minutes later, took him home for a ninety-minute rest, and then back to school for algebra.

Benjamin begged to return to school full time. We all knew—as parents, school staff, and doctors—that he wasn't yet ready. He was barely keeping up with his homework in the two classes. He wasn't exercising as he should, and he wasn't eating very much or drinking enough fluids. Maybe, we thought, returning to school would be motivation enough to get him to do the things necessary for him to get better.

Spring Break was the week of March 22. The doctor wrote an order giving Benjamin permission to return to school after break for four periods a day, essentially half-time, provided he complete his homework, exercise thirty minutes morning and afternoon as prescribed, and drink at least thirty-two ounces of fluids each day.

This was the motivation he needed. After Spring Break, he added social studies and science to his schedule. To conserve energy, he attended class in a wheelchair. Because of his required thirty-two ounces of fluid each day, he was allowed to keep a water bottle with him in each class.

Middle school years are especially difficult socially. It feels like everyone else belongs, but you are the odd man out. Differences often become the source of teasing or jealousy or both. Because Benjamin had a water bottle and other students didn't, the water bottle became a point of contention.

Even though Benjamin had missed nearly five months of school, he thought he could return to school, renew old relationships, and find his place once again among his peers. What he didn't understand was that while his life had been hijacked for the last five months, his classmates' relationships had continued to evolve. His place among his schoolmates had all but disappeared.

Those classmates didn't understand what was going on with Benjamin either. As an adult who'd walked with him on this GBS journey for nearly five months, there was a lot *I* didn't understand. So who could expect teenagers to understand? They thought he was getting preferential treatment, and it just wasn't fair. They'd see him in the wheelchair and then they'd see him walking, so they believed he used the wheelchair for attention.

We didn't know when to push Benjamin about his physical exertion. This is how it was explained to us: when healthy people get tired, they still have energy reserves they can draw from. Recovering GBS patient have no reserves. When their energy is depleted, they must rest.

We began referring to this energy situation as "Benjamin hitting a wall." The middle school students were confused. They'd see Benjamin walk from his wheelchair to his desk in one classroom.

Then in the next class he was unable to walk. It didn't make sense. He'd be fine in one class, so why did he get to go home to rest?

Struggling to survive at home, we weren't equipped to intervene in issues at school. Actually, at that time, we had little awareness of his stresses building there.

Church members looked for ways to support and encourage our family through this difficult time. It was often hard for them to know what to do. Benjamin's fourteenth birthday was on April 2. On the Sunday before his birthday, a group of people at church threw him a surprise birthday party after morning services. They had lunch, a cake, and a magician for entertainment. The party was a real encouragement and pick-me-up for him. He'd felt isolated for so long.

Much of March and April were a blur for Benjamin. The inability to remember, a side effect of his medication, was actually a blessing for him. Bootsie and I wished we could forget those months too. Because of her anxiety and depression, Bootsie went on medication too.

Benjamin had threatened to run away from home, and one afternoon he got on his bike and left. His mother was beside herself. Where did he go? Was he safe?

He had ridden to the associate pastor's house to talk. Pastor Alex's wife texted Bootsie to let her know Benjamin was with Alex and was safe. As long as Bootsie knew he was safe, she could relax a bit.

Benjamin continued to be very depressed. On one occasion, he opened his second-story window to jump. Scaring himself with what he'd just done, he came and told us.

This presented us with another dilemma. What should we do? Benjamin didn't want to go to the hospital. And I wasn't sure I'd know when it was time to go to the hospital. The guideline I'd always heard was that if he was a threat to himself or to others, he needed professional help. Benjamin wasn't threatening us. And as long as we were present with him, he wouldn't hurt himself.

On Wednesday night, Benjamin said he was in too much pain to go upstairs to his bed. He wanted to sleep on the couch. In his state of mind, we certainly wouldn't let him stay downstairs unsupervised. We unfolded the hide-a-bed in the game room for Benjamin and me. Bootsie, worried that I might not hear if Benjamin got up in the night, slept on the living-room couch just outside the door of the game room.

Thursday was a horrible day. Benjamin went to school only for one class and had physical therapy in the afternoon. Signs of depression were apparent to the physical therapist. She always charted objective information about Benjamin's treatment and progress, and she often noted subjective observations concerning his emotions. On Monday, she'd written that he didn't want to talk. On Thursday, he told her he'd tried to hurt himself on several occasions. She called Bootsie to confirm that we were aware of his emotional state.

My wife was relieved when I came home for dinner. The coming showdown would be easier to fight together than alone.

At dinner, Benjamin said he thought he needed some help. I asked him if he was willing to go to the hospital. He thought the hospital might help. He felt he just needed to take a week off from reality. Perhaps, he thought, this would be a vacation from home, and he'd be away from the pressures of school.

I knew this type of hospitalization would be very different from his previous hospitalizations. I think Benjamin expected it would be like the others; he was in for a rude awakening.

I knew he needed more help then we could provide at home. He'd given us an opening to seek treatment, and I didn't want to miss the opportunity.

Benjamin now feared going upstairs because of his thoughts of jumping. I stayed downstairs with him while Bootsie packed for a hospital stay for him and a hotel stay for the two of us.

Fortunately, we had good insurance. I'd become very familiar with the system's requirements when it came to a medical admission. A psychiatric admission was different. I assumed we'd be going to Indianapolis, but I didn't know which psychiatric units our insurance network covered.

I called our insurance's behavioral health hotline after 6:00 p.m. I explained that my son was suicidal and that I was calling to find the nearest in-network adolescent psychiatric unit.

The representative asked, "Is your son safe right now?"

I said, "Yes, he is safe right now, because I'm with him."

"Okay," was her reply. "You need to call back tomorrow during regular business hours between eight and five Central Time."

I felt my blood pressure shoot through the top of my head. *What?* She had no idea what we'd been through in the previous three days, let alone in the previous five months. Benjamin was safe only because I'd slept by his bedside the last three nights. She didn't understand what I knew: that taking him to the hospital would be a lot easier when he was agreeable than forcing him when he wasn't. I thought I'd done the right thing by contacting my insurance provider to make sure I went to an in-network provider. Instead, I was instructed to call back during regular business hours.

There was no reasoning with her. There were no other options. No matter what I said, her direction was always to call back tomorrow during regular business hours.

I was determined to do whatever I could to keep Benjamin safe for another night. Still, a dark thought crossed my mind: *If he makes a successful suicide attempt tonight, I'll have no reason to call in the morning.*

I was furious. I was doing the best I could for my son and my best to work within the guidelines of our insurance company, yet I was getting nowhere. When I asked to talk with a supervisor, no one was available. Again, I got the infuriating dismissal, "Call back during normal business hours."

I didn't know where to go. I'd thought my insurance company would at least tell me the location of an adolescent psychiatric unit. However, this customer service representative wouldn't even share that information with me.

We decided Indianapolis would be best, but at the time, I didn't know where we would go. Back to Peyton Manning Children's Hospital? Maybe another hospital?

While we were driving, I got a call from the insurance provider. This person, more experienced than the first, tried to make amends for my previous experience. She gave me names of two hospitals in Indianapolis in our behavioral health network. When I called each of the facilities, they told me they didn't have any available beds for a male adolescent. Each hospital empathized with our situation and gave me the number of another facility that might be able to help.

We knew there were concerns with the mental health system in our nation. Now, for the first time, we were experiencing the crisis firsthand. There are too few available beds to handle adolescent needs. Without insurance, we would have been looking at another set of obstacles.

I finally found a facility with an available bed for an adolescent male. It was in the Behavioral Health Unit at the St. Charles Hospital in Indianapolis. This was the only opening I could find, and it wasn't a part of our insurance network. It was interesting to learn that St. Charles Hospital was in-network for our medical insurance, but not for our behavioral health plan.

We decided that if St. Charles were the only opening, we'd go there and worry about insurance issues later. To be admitted to the behavioral health unit, Benjamin would need to go to the emergency room for possible admission.

We arrived at the emergency room of St. Charles Hospital at about 8:00 p.m. They called for a psychiatric consultation, and it was determined that Benjamin should be admitted to the Adolescent Behavioral Health Unit. It was after midnight when they finally escorted all of us from the emergency room to the locked unit.

When we arrived, it was quiet with the hallway lights off. Patients in the unit had already gone to bed. We all sat at a round table with one of the staff members answering many questions about our current crisis as well as the history of our GBS journey and our family background. Benjamin was taking sixteen different medications.

After thirty minutes, one of the staff members escorted him to his room to prepare for bed. Bootsie and I continued sitting at the table, answering questions and filling out papers. It was about 2:00 a.m. when we left the unit.

Since he was on suicide watch, staff pulled Benjamin's bed into the hallway in front of the nurse's station. Bootsie and I went across the street to stay in a hospital-affiliated hotel.

Early the next morning, we returned to the behavioral health unit to meet with the person coordinating Benjamin's care. She said the psychiatrist had already been in and had concerns about the number of medications he was on. He understood the purpose of the medications, but in light of side effects and the struggles Benjamin was facing, he judged it necessary to change his prescriptions. The coordinator said the psychiatrist would be in contact with Benjamin's neurologist to make adjustments. She also said they'd need to keep him under close supervision while the changes were being made.

We were allowed to see Benjamin for a few minutes. This hospitalization was nothing like anything he'd experienced before. He didn't want to be there. When he begged us to take him home, we had to refuse. We knew he needed close supervision as they changed his medications. He needed to be in the hospital.

He became very angry, lashing out. "If you're not going to take me home, then just leave."

That's what we did, as hard as it was. We told him that we loved him, and then we left. That was probably the most difficult thing we had ever done. Bootsie was crying as we walked out the door. We knew it was where he needed to be, but that didn't make it any easier. We were also terrified by the thought that we'd never again have a relationship with our son as we'd had before he contracted GBS. He was now a different person. Would we ever again see the kind, gentle spirit of our son?

We sent Benjamin's name through the church prayer chain. When he was dealing with the physical symptoms of GBS, it had been easier to share specifics of his condition. With the psychiatric admission, we didn't feel as comfortable sharing details.

In our culture, it's acceptable to be in a hospital for physical reasons. However, a psychiatric admission isn't viewed the same way. We wanted people to pray, yet we also wanted to protect Benjamin's privacy. So we didn't share about depression or suicide threats; we did say the doctors were adjusting his medications. That was true, and it was also true that medications were a contributing factor to his emotional state.

Benjamin was angry and uncooperative. Each day, the staff offered him an opportunity to promise not to hurt himself. Every day he refused. As a result, he continued to sleep in front of the nurse's station. Anger toward his mother and me continued to escalate.

We visited him on Saturday afternoon. Once again, he asked us to take him home. We said we couldn't do it. We explained that he needed to be there until the doctors dismissed him.

He said he hated us and that we should just go home.

We told him we loved him. We honored his request, and again we left. Our visit had lasted only ten minutes. We had traveled about ninety minutes, one way, to visit. Regardless of what our son said, he needed to know that he was loved. He needed to hear that we were there for him and would walk with him through this recovery.

We didn't visit him on Sunday. But every weekday evening we traveled to Indianapolis to see him during the family visiting hour at 6:30 p.m.

Benjamin slept in front of the nurse's station five nights before he agreed not to hurt himself. On the fifth day, he realized he wouldn't get out of the unit until he started cooperating. He didn't engage in the program because he wanted to; he saw his cooperation as the only way he'd be discharged.

During his hospital stay, they discontinued three medications and changed two others. They discontinued the ones that seemed to be having the greatest psychiatric side effects.

Benjamin wasn't willing to open up about his anger because of GBS. Or his fears. Or his relational struggles at school. Adjusting his medications was probably the biggest accomplishment of the hospitalization, a necessary and important step.

Benjamin's case manager gave us an article to read by Robert J. Gregory, PhD, "Recovery from Depression Associated with Guillain-Barré Syndrome." We'd done a lot of reading about GBS, but this was the first information we'd encountered about GBS's emotional impact. Dr. Gregory wrote, "The emotional impact is often profound, both for patient and for family members."

Was that ever true! And what a relief! It was so nice to read an article, published by a school of psychology, confirming what we'd experienced. Dr. Gregory also acknowledged that much research had been done on the physiological aspects of GBS, but very little on the psychosocial aspects of the disease. He identified psychosocial elements including weakness, pain, fatigue, and depression. Benjamin was dealing with all of these, and they were affecting his recovery.

Our son was discouraged and confused by these issues. As parents, we were frustrated because we didn't know when to push harder or when to back off. Friends, who weren't able to understand, just thought he should get over it.

The staff was in tune with the psychological stresses that come with a long-term recovery. Benjamin still had an intense fear of a relapse, though cognitively, he knew a relapse was unlikely. Nevertheless, every pain or change in his body reactivated fears of a relapse. His case psychologist tested for post-traumatic stress disorder (PTSD). Based on criteria used to diagnose PTSD, Benjamin was one symptom away from that diagnosis.

During his hospital admission, we attended two family therapy sessions. We worried they'd tell us what horrible parents we were and what we needed to do differently. While they didn't "beat us up" during these sessions, we as parents still felt very vulnerable, certain that we were failures.

After a week in the behavioral health unit, Benjamin was ready to be released. The doctors described him as having cognitive dulling. The dictionary defines cognitive dulling as "trouble remembering, difficulty remembering or learning new things, and difficulty in concentrating and making decisions that affect everyday life." This seemed to describe our son's condition accurately.

Chapter 13

Slow Progress

Benjamin desperately wanted to return to school full time. Again, he wasn't ready. Physically he didn't have the stamina to attend all day. The behavioral health staff had noted he struggled with peer relationships and that he was overwhelmed by his inability to adjust to change.

When discharged from the hospital, he was taking only thirteen prescriptions. He said a fog had lifted after he was off some of his medicines. He was thankful to be thinking a little clearer.

Now he had another fear: that the intense neuropathy pain would return. He thought since it took all the medications to stop the neuropathy pain, without the medications, pain would undoubtedly return. Understandably, Benjamin was determined never to deal with that type of intense pain again. Some of his pain medicine was to be taken as needed. Every time he had any pain, he could request a pain pill.

There were six weeks left in the school year. Benjamin would take only three classes: social studies, English, and algebra. He would arrive in the morning at school with all the other students. He'd attend social studies and English classes, which were first and second hour. Then, after a ninety-minute rest at home, he'd go back to school for algebra.

During the time Benjamin was in the hospital, a friend's college-aged son died unexpectedly. All I could think was "That could have been my son." The two losses seemed to merge. I believe that, in some way, I was also grieving the loss of my son. I didn't know the circumstances around my friend's loss, but I grieved with him and felt compelled to go to his son's funeral. I wanted to show support to my friend and his family, but this also became a way for me to deal with my own grief.

Benjamin was doing better physically. He could run short distances and was able to walk longer distances. The 5K run was on Saturday, May 8, and we'd looked forward to it for many weeks. With the training I'd been undertaking, I knew I could complete 3.1 miles.

Since contracting GBS, Benjamin hadn't yet gone that distance. I'd decided I would carry him across the finish line, if necessary. Our plan was to jog a block and walk a block.

It was a cool May morning in Indianapolis, which made it more comfortable to run. Our time wasn't important. The goal was to finish the race *together*.

We did just that.

After all we'd been through, this was a huge victory. Benjamin was doing much better with his recovery. I'd progressed from not being able to run a quarter of a mile to running 3.1 miles. Even though I didn't run 3.1 miles on race day, I could have. That was a major accomplishment for me.

It was Mother's Day weekend. We had decided I'd take a vacation day on Sunday, and we'd spend the weekend in Indianapolis. We'd have a relaxing family weekend together, something we desperately needed.

After the race, we got Benjamin back to the hotel room, and he took a long nap. He just wanted to stay in the room. He was completely depleted and just wanted to rest. Nevertheless, our weekend was a great success.

As the school year ended, the eighth-grade class took a trip to Washington, DC. This was a popular trip for eighth-graders and a good culminating experience to their middle school years.

Before he contracted GBS, we'd registered Benjamin for the trip. We'd always been optimistic that life would be back to normal in time for him to take the trip. The closer the time came, however, the more we were aware that he couldn't keep up with the rigorous schedule. He'd need more sleep than most of the other students. Obviously a plan was needed that allowed his needs to be met, without becoming an obstacle for everyone else on the trip.

Benjamin just wanted to be normal. He wanted to be able to do what other kids his age were doing. But the simple fact was, he couldn't. We talked with the sponsor of the trip about whether his needs could be met, and she was willing to try. We agreed on a plan, which included us paying for a responsible graduating senior to attend as Benjamin's personal chaperone. The two of them would participate in everything with the other students. They would share a room, allowing Benjamin to get more sleep at night. We'd also provide the chaperone with taxi money so they could go back to the hotel whenever Benjamin was too tired to keep up with the group.

Benjamin went on the trip and enjoyed it. He'd missed many activities during his eighth-grade year, but this trip was an excellent culmination of his middle school experience.

Even though the trip was a success in many ways, it may have fostered more tension between Benjamin and a few of his classmates. Some students viewed his accommodations as unnecessary special treatment. For example, when the group visited the US Capitol Building, Benjamin was given a ride on a golf cart. Everyone else had to climb over one hundred steps up to the Capitol. At the time, we had believed Benjamin's participation on this trip was a positive way to reconnect with some of his peers. In retrospect, it may have done just the opposite.

At the end of June, Benjamin went to a week of summer church camp at Epworth Forest in northern Indiana. He loved church camp and had gone since first grade. He'd also attended other camps with me over the years. And he'd been at Epworth Forest when, in years gone by, I was in charge of a cabin. Now this would be his first time as a camper.

During the week, he struggled with stamina. He was much better than he'd been just a month earlier on the eighth-grade trip, but he was far from being able to keep up with all the demands of camp.

The first two afternoons, he went to the game field to take part in activities with the other campers. He was able to participate, but he was exhausted the rest of the day. He slept through the evening program and through Prayer and Share, the closing worship time in the cabin. If he slept during the afternoon, he could stay awake for more of the evening worship times. Yet even an afternoon nap didn't give him enough stamina to stay up late with the other campers. It became an ongoing joke that whenever someone couldn't find Benjamin, all they had to do was look on his bed. He'd be there—sound asleep.

Benjamin had had high expectations for the week of camp, but it was tougher than he expected. He looked fine, but physical endurance was an issue.

Relationally he struggled to reconnect with his friends. Everyone's life had changed in the last six to eight months. He wanted relationships to be just as they'd been prior to GBS. But his recovery was taking too long. His patience was wearing thin. He was frustrated—even angry—that no one understood what had happened to him and was still happening.

Because his world had come crashing down and he hadn't been able to put it back together, Benjamin also faced a crisis of faith. Sometimes a crisis of faith and blaming God is a season a person passes through. Unfortunately, some people stay in that place of bitterness and blaming God the rest of their lives. In Psalm 23:4, the psalmist wrote, "Even though I walk through the valley of the shadow of death, I will fear no evil." The valley can be a dark, dangerous, and scary place, but there is good news. God doesn't want us to stay in the valley. He wants to walk with us as we pass through the valley.

Why would God put him through this? Benjamin was mad at God. He told us later of praying more in that week of camp than he'd ever prayed in his life. He wanted answers! He wanted them now!

Nevertheless, answers didn't come.

We often want immediate answers or resolutions to our problems. We want to get on with life. We want to get back to doing what we want to do. Sometimes what seems like a delay is actually a time when God is shaping and molding us into who he wants us to be.

During the summer of 2010, Benjamin made more progress. Doctors slowly decreased his medications. He had increased stamina but still required a lot of sleep.

One of Benjamin's childhood goals was visiting each of the continental states before graduating high school. In the summer of 2010, we flew to Las Vegas, Nevada, rented a car, and drove to five other states in the southwest. Spending a lot of time in the car suited Benjamin just fine. He'd sleep in the back seat. When we made a stop, he'd briefly get out of the car, get right back in, and take another nap. Without much exertion, he marked six states off his goal list.

The only part of the trip that was more than he could take was Las Vegas. One day, we walked to see the sites on the Las Vegas strip. The temperature was over a hundred degrees, which was normal for Las Vegas but not for us. As we headed back to the hotel, Benjamin was exhausted. He protested, "I can't walk any further." He'd hit the proverbial wall. He wasn't paralyzed as he'd been in the hospital; he could stand, but he couldn't keep going. On that evening there was no energy and no reserves. Our hotel was in sight, but he could walk no further. We flagged down a cab.

The trip was a good change of pace for all of us, but decisions had to be made every day based on Benjamin's needs and limitations.

No matter how much we may have wanted to forget about GBS, we couldn't escape its effects.

Despite his ongoing times of depression and adolescent self-centeredness when he couldn't see beyond what he wanted, there were also times when Benjamin felt compelled to help others. One of his altruistic thoughts was to help the GBS/CIDP Foundation International. The mission of the foundation is to provide support, education, research, and advocacy for individuals and families affected by GBS or CIDP. It had been an excellent source of information and encouragement for us as we learned more about Benjamin's diagnosis. We thought this positive investment during his summer vacation could also lift some of his depression. Benjamin's idea was to conduct a fundraising event for the foundation. He decided on a 5K run, pancake breakfast, and silent auction. His theme for the event was "Defeat GBS Around the World."

Bootsie and I happily gave him help and advice. The local radio station helped publicize the event. Volunteers at church helped with the breakfast. Benjamin did most of the organizational work. He wrote letters, met with sponsors, and did radio and television interviews. His effort raised awareness of GBS in the area and over $5,000 for the national foundation. We were immensely proud of him.

Benjamin continued to get stronger over the summer. His endurance was better, although he still slept a lot. He preferred being inactive to being active. Was this GBS, or was it because he was a teenager? Throughout Benjamin's recovery, it was always hard to know what was GBS and what was another factor in his life. GBS certainly wasn't the direct cause of all Benjamin's struggles, but it presented extenuating circumstances that made his issues more difficult.

Chapter 14

Fresh Start

As his freshman year in high school approached, Benjamin looked forward to beginning a new school year. He expected a fresh start and a successful high school career. However, as much as he wanted everything to be back to normal, it wasn't.

We talked with his guidance counselor, the school nurse, and all of his teachers; they said they would do whatever they could to accommodate Benjamin's needs. If he needed to leave class early and take a nap to make it through the rest of the day, he'd go to the nurse's office. Everyone was very cooperative. Everyone wanted Benjamin to succeed.

Most high school freshmen took a physical education class. As Benjamin needed to be strategic about where he expended his energy throughout the day, that could wait until his sophomore year. He'd been selected to be a part of the high school show choir, but they did choreography. He wasn't ready for that level of activity, so he transferred to another choir. The show choir would have to wait another year. His guidance counselor also adjusted his schedule so he'd have a study hall as a strategic break in the middle of the day.

While in middle school, he'd never officially dropped out of band class, but he never returned after his eighth-grade hospitalizations. The high school band started the school year marching. Marching band required long rehearsals, not just during the school day but also outside of school hours. Benjamin didn't have the strength or the stamina to participate.

Most members of the band marched, but there was a group of percussionists who didn't. They stood in "the pit," an area in front of the band on the side of the field. In addition to playing the clarinet, Benjamin played piano. The director asked him if he'd play keyboard in the pit, rather than march on the field. This change allowed our son to continue participating with the band.

However, rehearsals were still long. Everyone became tired. The others pushed on to do what was required, but Benjamin, still recovering from GBS, didn't have the reserve energy to push through. He did just enough to get by. This necessary tactic didn't endear him to other students. His high school career wasn't getting off to a good start.

The first week of school wasn't bad, but when the weekend arrived, he was exhausted. He did what he could to rest, but he went into the new week tired. Week two involved more homework. Exhausted, he'd come home from school and not want to do homework. His spirits had been better over the summer, but now he was sinking again into a dark place.

"The darkest place in my life" is how Benjamin later described this time. Once again, the stresses of homework were building, and he was struggling with relationships. He felt isolated and alone. This was another catch-22. Every time he took advantage of accommodations made for him, it caused greater tension with his peers. The greater the relationship struggle with his peers, the more depressed he became. As his depression increased, more accommodations were necessary.

During the second week of classes, he didn't make it through a full school day. He complained of increasing pain. On Tuesday, the doctor ordered lab work and an X-ray because of pain in his spine and some difficulty breathing. Nothing of significance was identified.

By Friday, the pain was such that Bootsie called the pediatrician's office more than once. Dr. Padgett realized that a medicine for nerve pain had been slowly decreased since his April hospitalization. As it turned out, this medicine had been discontinued the same week school started, which was probably not the best timing. Dr. Padgett re-prescribed two medications that had been effective in treating his pain in the past.

When approaching the end of a day, I'd often breathe a sigh of relief. We'd made it through another day.

Bedtime was when our son would have the most irrational meltdowns. (This was how I thought of them, as they seemed to come unprovoked.) Benjamin was tired of dealing with his recovery. He was depressed, and he had little desire to live. He talked about suicide again. His plan was to jump out of his second-story bedroom window. He didn't try it because he reasoned that if he did, he'd only hurt himself and not actually die.

I slept on the floor next to his bed that weekend. As I remember those nights on the floor, I wonder how many other parents have done something similar to keep their child safe. As a parent, you do what you must for your child's well-being.

On Monday morning, he refused to go to school. He was in pain and depressed. Bootsie called Dr. Padgett for an appointment, and we both went with him. The pediatrician examined him, noting his high levels of pain. He observed that Benjamin was apathetic and had lost focus and motivation. "He wants to be a normal kid, but he wants to kill himself because he can't be normal," Dr. Padgett's observed.

Benjamin had told Dr. Padgett that he planned to jump out a window and had threatened to starve himself to death. Dr. Padgett couldn't allow us to take him home; he needed another psychiatric admission.

I thought, *Here we go again.* I knew we couldn't return to the St. Charles Behavioral Health Unit, because it was out of our insurance network. Memorial Central, another hospital in the Indianapolis area, was in our network. Dr. Padgett's office called to verify that they had an adolescent male bed available. We went directly to the hospital for further evaluation and possible admission.

Memorial Central conducted their initial evaluation and determined that Benjamin needed inpatient treatment. As we waited, I observed the plight of other patients being evaluated. Despite hospital privacy guidelines, I could hear conversations with other patients. I saw a pattern. Patients with insurance coverage were processed for admission. Those without insurance were being assisted in finding a ride home. My heart went out to the families and individuals who felt as helpless as we did. Many of them wouldn't receive any assistance. I don't comment as a criticism of the hospital; this was simply another example of our broken and inadequate mental health system.

After receiving insurance approval, Benjamin was admitted to the adolescent unit with diagnoses of severe depressive disorder and severe anxiety. Benjamin continued to be worried about a relapse of GBS. Even though PTSD had been ruled out in April, they would again consider PTSD as a diagnosis. As our son entered the hospital, he was on fourteen medications.

Again, we wanted to send Benjamin's name through the church prayer chain. What would we say this time? We still didn't want to share that he was suicidal—though he was. We didn't want to say he was an emotional basket case—though he was. We said that Benjamin was in the Memorial Central Hospital to monitor needed changes in his medications and that he was having a difficult time with the beginning of a new school year.

After making this prayer request, I was surprised by the number of parents in the church who talked with me about emotional struggles they'd had with their teenagers. While the stories they shared may have happened ten or fifteen years earlier, they could read between the lines of what I'd said.

As they spoke about their experiences with their teenager, their eyes would often brim with tears as they confessed, "I've never told anyone what we went through."

How sad. In the church, we say we want to care for one another, yet when families go through their darkest times, they often suffer alone. Sometimes this lonely anguish comes because others don't reach out. Other times it happens because the family doesn't allow others to comfort and care for them.

We tried to be open about our experiences, but it was easier to share them when we were dealing with physical symptoms. We felt we should be more protective of the details of his emotional journey. Our concern for his privacy was genuine, but there was also a level of personal pride or embarrassment involved. It is socially acceptable to share about a physical illness, but there is often a stigma with mental or emotional illness.

Stigma follows mental illness, and it's harder to talk about because often there is no predictable path to recovery. When one is recovering from a physical illness or a surgery, there is often a somewhat predictable path to wholeness. When dealing with emotional issues, one never knows when the next hill or valley is going to throw life into a tailspin.

We were struggling. We knew people cared about us. They wanted to help, but they didn't know what to do. We didn't know what we needed.

Bootsie communicated with a college friend about our struggles. Her friend's response was like that of so many people: "I have tried several times to find the right words to say to you, but I didn't know what to say. So I have said nothing." Her honesty wasn't unkind or hurtful. She expressed what so many felt, and we understood.

Benjamin had lost his motivation to excel in school, something new for him. Still, despite his loss of academic motivation, a source of stress at Memorial Central was that they limited patients to one hour of homework per day. Benjamin was anxious about several things, and this new inability to work on his homework intensified his anxiety to a new level.

The Behavioral Health Unit at St. Charles had seemed to understand Benjamin's need for additional rest because of his GBS history. Memorial Central, on the other hand, wouldn't allow him to take naps. They didn't believe he needed them. In retrospect, we witnessed him needing extra rest for nearly two years following the onset of GBS. Was this need for rest because of GBS? Was it because of adolescence? Or was it a way to escape? These rule limiting homework and sleep only amplified Benjamin's sense of having no control in his life. He felt like he was in prison.

Benjamin was discharged from Memorial Central on Friday. They'd stopped one medicine and added three more to his regimen. Once again, they found he didn't quite fit a diagnosis of PTSD. His diagnoses remained severe major depressive disorder and anxiety disorder.

Even though he'd been working on a monthly basis with the outpatient psychology clinic at BHC, the doctors recommended that he establish a weekly relationship with a therapist in the Lafayette area. In fact, they wouldn't dismiss him until we confirmed his first appointment.

It was hard for me to hold on to hope. I wanted to be optimistic. I would, of course, continue to do all I could to help my son become healthy again. However, I began to ask, "What if nothing changes? What if this is the new normal for our family?" It was a horrifying thought. What kept me going was remembering God's faithfulness in days gone by.

I believed Benjamin was a gift to Bootsie and me, as most parents feel about their children. Fifteen years earlier, we had gone through infertility treatments. The treatments included medical testing, surgery, medication, artificial insemination, and in vitro fertilization. All failed. The journey of infertility was a roller coaster ride, and we had decided in the beginning that we would go as far as in vitro fertilization, but we would do it only one time. That decision was made because of finances as well as emotional considerations.

There was a point at which enough was enough. After one failed attempt of in vitro fertilization, we told our doctor that we were ending treatments. He told us there was little to no chance we would ever be able to achieve a pregnancy, adding, "Conceiving would be nothing short of a miracle."

In less than six months of the failed in vitro attempt and the death of that dream, Benjamin was conceived. We believed that he was a gift from God. Because of God's faithfulness in the past, I could trust God with the future. Even if the future wasn't going to look like what I anticipated, I could trust him.

If this was our new normal, I also believed God would provide the strength and perseverance we needed to get through. There are many families coping with the consequences of mental illness. It was certainly not something I desired, but we were no more or less deserving of such a cross to bear than anyone else.

Chapter 15

Sick and Tired

The high school used block scheduling, which meant students had only four classes a day. One day they'd have four classes, and the next day they'd have a different four classes. While Benjamin liked block scheduling, sitting in a school desk for an hour and forty minutes was a physical challenge.

The discomfort in his back and legs from neuropathy continued, though the sharp, shooting pain was controlled by medications. Teachers and the guidance department continued to work with him to find a workable schedule. For example, his thinking was clearer first thing in the morning, so he attended mentally challenging classes in first or second periods. A nap after lunch renewed his strength for the final class of the day.

Later, Benjamin would remember ten schedule changes. His mother would remember changing the schedule on our home bulletin board about every other day.

Over the course of the first few weeks of the semester, the doctors recommended several accommodations to be made at school. He needed a cushion to sit on, because the seats were hard and caused leg discomfort that led to nerve firings. A footstool raised his feet during class and also helped alleviate leg discomfort. He was to walk around in the back of the classroom if he needed to move because of the long class periods. He had a filled water bottle to increase his fluid intake. And finally, if needed, he would be allowed to go to the nurse's office to take a nap.

Teachers and school administrators genuinely wanted to help Benjamin succeed. And these accommodations were physically helpful for him even though they caused relational problems with other students. The common opinion of students seemed to be that Benjamin was faking it. They believed he was getting unfair advantages that he didn't deserve and, even worse, were unnecessary. As we worked to navigate his recovery—no easy task—Benjamin felt isolated and alone. None of his peers understood, and he was having a difficult time reestablishing friendships.

At home, Benjamin used texting and social media. I think he spent too much time attempting to justify his actions and explain his needs. In the end, he didn't convince anyone, which did nothing to advance his cause.

Because of the GBS/CIDP benefit he'd organized before school started, he'd become Facebook friends with other GBS survivors. Those relationships were generally positive and encouraging. However, one wasn't. One Facebook friend wrote, "If you try too hard, you will get worse."

That was just what Benjamin wanted to hear: a reason to stop trying. Eventually we contacted that person and asked her to stop communicating with him. Our observation was that texting and social media helped Benjamin feel less isolated. But sometimes those media were detrimental to his recovery and emotional state.

After his last hospitalization, Benjamin began seeing a therapist at a clinic in Lafayette. Laura wasn't only a therapist; she was also a clinical nurse specialist who used Christian principles in her practice.

They met weekly and established a trusting relationship. She provided techniques to calm his fears and anxieties. However, after about four weeks, his depression and anxieties began intensifying.

The marching band rehearsed every Wednesday evening. Benjamin's energy level was so low by that time of day he was excused from the evening rehearsals. At the beginning of October, I convinced him to push himself and go to an evening rehearsal. The marching band, nearing its sectional competition, was working hard to polish the show. Everyone needed to be present. I took Benjamin to the rehearsal and sat in the stands to watch.

After an hour, he walked over to me and said, "I have to go."

I told him I really wanted him to stay; I knew it was an important rehearsal.

"I just can't do it any more tonight," he countered. On the way to the car, out of the sight of the band, he fell to the ground, crying. I was surprised and perplexed. Was this physical exhaustion or an emotional meltdown?

Not long after arriving home, Benjamin received a phone call from his section leader, a student, demanding to know why he left practice early. He was calling from the football field where the band was still practicing, obviously frustrated. But it was also apparent he had no idea what we were experiencing. It was another indication that tensions at school were intensifying.

As the week went on, I was again sleeping at his bedside.

On the following Monday appointment with Laura, he told her that he'd attempted suicide the night before. He'd hit himself in the head with a heavy rock and tied a drawstring from his pajamas around his neck. Both attempts were in the bathroom. All of this was news to us. Bootsie was numb. We were both so beat down at that point that we hardly had a response left in us.

Laura had no choice but to recommend another psychiatric admission. In a private conversation with Bootsie, the two of them agreed on a plan. The therapist would arrange for admission, and Bootsie would return home with Benjamin to pack and to get me. Benjamin wouldn't be told he'd be hospitalized until I got home and we were ready to leave.

When we told Benjamin that he'd be admitted again to Memorial Central, he ran into the game room, locked himself in, and firmly declared he wasn't going.

Talking through the door and rationalizing got us nowhere. Eventually I got the door unlocked. Now that we were in the same room, he resorted to physical threats against me. He held a pool stick to use as a weapon. He never actually struck me, but in his desperation, he didn't know what else to do.

Benjamin continued to insist that he wouldn't go to the hospital. We insisted that he had no choice. He was small enough that I could have forcefully put him in the car, but I certainly didn't want to do that.

Since his therapist had required the admission, I knew I could call the police and an ambulance would probably be called to transport him to Memorial Central. When I explained this possibility, Benjamin reluctantly agreed to get in the car.

Because of his emotional state and our worries, we changed the setting on the back car doors so they could be opened only from the outside.

It was a long drive to the hospital in Indianapolis.

At the hospital, he refused to get out of the car. A security guard escorted him inside. At admission, Benjamin was identified as a nine on the ten-point suicide scale.

He had continued to deal with the same issues: major depressive disorder, severe anxiety, stress keeping up in school, problems with friends at school, and anxiety about a relapse of GBS. It was even noted on his chart that his parents felt hopeless.

We had been through so much as a family. Would it ever end? As a parent, a father, I just wanted to take his pain away. But I couldn't. In Proverbs 13:12, Solomon wrote, "Hope deferred makes the heart sick, but a longing fulfilled is a tree of life." How right Solomon was. With no hope in sight, my heart was sick. No light at the end of the tunnel. No end in sight. Even though I didn't know how we were ever going to make it through, my faith never wavered. Even as life circumstances weren't as I hoped, I believed God would see us through.

Entering the hospital, Benjamin was taking eight prescriptions. During the hospitalization, they discontinued two and added one. He was on only seven medications when he was discharged.

Benjamin had learned the ropes of the behavioral health unit. The sooner he did what they wanted him to do, the sooner he'd get out. He was discharged by noon on Friday.

Emotionally he was in a better place, but the stressors in his life were the same. Plus, he was now another week behind in school. Relationships had been avoided for a week, but nothing had improved. His intense fear of a relapse also remained.

Benjamin's behavioral health admissions were primarily triage to get him through the crisis and past the danger of hurting himself. Long-term improvement would come through ongoing counseling and therapy. Upon discharge, the recommendation was that Benjamin attend an intensive outpatient program at the Adolescent Stress Center in Indianapolis. This meant a ninety-minute one-way drive, three days a week for four weeks. It also entailed missing more school. This was a major expense and heavy time commitment. But we knew we had no choice: we had to do something. Hospitalization every four to six weeks wasn't a viable option.

Benjamin continued meeting with Laura every week. He didn't seem angry with her for sending him back to Memorial Central. She was familiar with the recommended program at the Stress Center and thought it would be helpful for him. Getting insurance approval took about two weeks, and he was accepted into the next group.

When he was in his second week of the outpatient program at the stress center, Benjamin woke up unable to move from the waist down. It was November 11, 2010. I carried him downstairs. We moved him around in his wheelchair. Until then, he'd used the wheelchair only when he was extremely tired.

Bootsie called the pediatrician's office for an appointment, and they asked that we bring him right in. Back we went to the hospital for testing. Home Hospital had closed since Benjamin's last admission and had merged with another hospital. Because of insurance coverage, he was admitted to the Lafayette Regional Medical Center. This would be his tenth hospitalization at six different hospitals in just over a year. I couldn't help but wonder if we might be investigated by child protective services because of the number of different hospitals to which we had taken him. There was a good reason for each admission, but that was a lot of facilities.

This hospital did X-rays and lab work. The neurologist examined him and conducted an EMG. The conclusion was that whatever was going on in his body, it wasn't a relapse of GBS. This huge relief for us as parents also meant Benjamin's biggest fear wasn't substantiated. He'd had a mild case of the stomach flu over the weekend, and he'd remembered being told that sometimes having the flu can trigger GBS. He'd been positive this paralysis was a relapse.

As the pediatrician talked to Benjamin about his journey with GBS, he realized that the original diagnosis of GBS had been made one year earlier—to the very week. As they talked, Benjamin said, "I'm not mad at my mother anymore for making me get the flu vaccine." That was a change. For months he'd blamed it all on Bootsie.

Benjamin may have forgiven his mother, but that didn't mean she had forgiven herself. She still felt guilty. Now, if Benjamin no longer blamed her, maybe it would be easier to stop blaming herself.

Benjamin was diagnosed with conversion disorder. Mayo Clinic explains it this way: "Conversion disorder, also called functional neurological symptom disorder, is a condition in which you show psychological stress in physical ways." He didn't have a relapse of GBS. His anxiety caused his body to convert his fears into paralysis similar to what he'd experienced during the acute stage of GBS. Conversion disorder is real, not imagined, and is often experienced by those who feel powerless. This disorder has been documented in other recovering GBS patients as well, though it's not limited to them.

Sue Baier, a GBS survivor and the author of *Bed Number 10*, wrote that her anxiety caused her to believe she was having a relapse. When the anxiety passed, so did her symptoms. For Benjamin, conversion disorder was a physical response mimicking the tingling and paralysis of GBS. So stress or anxiety would trigger his conversion disorder. When the stress and anxiety passed, the tingling would subside, and he'd regain his mobility.

Unassisted, Benjamin walked out of the hospital on Friday afternoon. Since he now knew he wasn't having a relapse, we hoped the conversion disorder would be over as well. This wasn't the case. Tingling in his extremities and weakness to the degree he couldn't walk became his body's physical response to the stresses of schoolwork and relational tensions.

After the November hospitalization, Benjamin rarely made it through a full day of school. Bootsie dreaded the phone ringing, fearing it was the school calling to report a problem or to ask her to pick him up early from school. Just as Bootsie experienced a shot of anxiety when the phone rang, my texting twitch became worse. Every time my phone vibrated with a text, a shot of adrenalin hit my body. I automatically assumed it was my wife sharing bad news.

Everyone was sick and tired.

Benjamin was tired of being sick and tired. He just wanted it all to be behind him. Physically, he was doing better, but he still tired easily. Relationally he felt isolated and that no one understood. Before GBS, school had been a place where he excelled. Now, in the midst of all the challenges, he couldn't find his way.

As parents, we were worn out. How much longer could we go on? It felt like we were at the absolute end of our rope. But walking away wasn't an option.

One evening, Benjamin was downstairs crying, and Bootsie was upstairs crying. She wanted me to mediate the problem. I told her, "I can't take on any more of the emotional load from you and Benjamin. I'm sorry that I can't lighten your load, but I feel like I'm just barely holding on by my fingernails."

I was at a breaking point. No longer could I hold everyone together. Maybe it was a point of resignation for me that I was incapable of doing this on my own. I had always depended on God during the journey. But on that night, I reached a new level of dependence. God may provide what we need, but that doesn't necessarily mean He provides reserves. He gives us what we need for each day, and in some cases, He gives us what we need for each moment. This was one of those "moment" occasions.

Some adults at school were fed up. They'd been very patient and willing to accommodate Benjamin's needs, but no degree of help got him through a full day of school. At the beginning of the school year, his guidance counselor had told him, "You don't have to worry about anything; I'll have your back." But Benjamin had lost trust in that relationship. He didn't feel anyone had his back. The school had legitimate reasons to be frustrated. The other side of the story was that when Benjamin felt abandoned, he also felt more desperate.

His friends and other students had all but written him off. The consensus was that for a long time Benjamin had been faking his condition. They believed he'd been getting unfair privileges, and he'd taken advantage of the situation. Of course, there were times when he should have handled some things differently. Nevertheless, his peers didn't understand the extent of his illness or what he was experiencing. As his parents, we didn't understand it all, so how could we expect others to understand? For over a year, this situation had been going on. It was time to move on.

If only it were that easy.

Chapter 16

Making a Change

The doctor's office must have dreaded hearing Bootsie's voice over the phone. But they never let on. They were always professional and genuinely concerned. Even when they received multiple calls in a given week or a given day, they tried to listen objectively and advise wisely. When others were frustrated and just wanted to put the whole matter behind them, Dr. Padgett and his staff were patient and persevered.

In December, just over one week before the end of the semester, Bootsie got a call from school to pick him up. Benjamin was unable to walk.

It was a snowy, slushy day, and she didn't think she had enough strength to get him in the car. So I went to pick him up.

Normally Benjamin could provide some assistance by standing. Once helped to his feet, he could pivot and sit down on the car seat. On this day, he couldn't stand at all. I positioned the wheelchair near the opened car door. Then I had to lift all his weight, unassisted, into the car. When we arrived home, Benjamin was completely dependent on me to get him out of the car and into the house.

Since the conversion disorder diagnosis, when he had a physical problem, our practice was to talk through his day to identify what triggered his body's response. On this day, it quickly became apparent the problem was an English assignment. The assignment was answering essay questions about *To Kill a Mockingbird*. This assignment served as the final in that class. He'd read the book but hadn't liked it. The assignment had twenty questions, and each answer was to fill half a page. The solution seemed to be that Benjamin needed to complete the assignment, and his stress would be relieved.

I took him to the dining room table to write. As he sat there, his paralysis got worse. He complained of tingling in his arms and hands. We continued to encourage him to keep writing. He complained of getting weaker, and in a matter of thirty minutes, he couldn't even hold his pencil.

Normally Benjamin worked independently on his homework. Now he obviously required help. Since he couldn't move his arms or legs, sitting in a straight-back chair was hard for him. I took him into the family room and laid him down on the couch.

Since he couldn't write, we said he could dictate his answers to his mother. He wasn't excited about this idea, but he needed to get the assignment finished and his stress relieved. When they finished, Bootsie went to the computer and typed what he'd said.

Over the next two hours, Benjamin's tingling began to subside, and he could move again. By the end of the evening, no evidence remained of the physical problems of the afternoon.

The semester ended just before Christmas. While it hadn't been the semester of high school Benjamin had hoped it would be, he'd survived. During Christmas vacation, he didn't have to worry about homework or stresses from school. It was a good two weeks around our home. Respite from all the drama was nice. We thought maybe we'd turned a corner and the next semester would be better.

On Monday, he had an appointment with his pediatrician. Dr. Padgett took a firmer approach, telling Benjamin, "You will go to school, and you will stay."

On Tuesday, he returned to school for the first day of the new semester. His guidance counselor (who had communicated with his pediatrician) told him that he wasn't to come down to the nurse's office or call home. Or have anyone call home on his behalf, except in the case of an emergency.

After school, Benjamin had an appointment with his therapist in Lafayette. He talked with Laura about the new semester and his stresses. Since homework hadn't yet started, relational stresses were the topic of conversation. They talked about coping strategies. Benjamin shared that the more people pushed him, the more he felt backed into a corner and as if he had no control. During these times, he felt powerless and his conversion disorder kicked in.

Benjamin went to school on Wednesday, but on Thursday he attended in a wheelchair. His mother reported leg weakness and tingling in his feet and ankles to the pediatrician's office. They instructed her to monitor him, and if it got worse, to bring him in. After coming home from school on Thursday, he took a nap. When he awoke, he couldn't walk. At about six, we headed again to the emergency room.

The emergency room doctor consulted with the pediatrician and admitted him to the hospital. The pediatrician had given instructions that Benjamin was to have no access to TV, his cell phone, or any other electronic devices. Obviously, Benjamin was not happy with this order.

Around nine he was taken to his room. He was angry with us. He was angry with the doctor. He was angry at the world.

We left at ten with him unable to move his legs in his bed and with his cell phone in our possession. Benjamin later reflected that if he'd been faking it that night, he would have followed us out the door. He felt helpless and alone.

While we didn't ordinarily read Benjamin's text conversations, we'd noticed a definite mood change while he waited and texted in the emergency room. We were searching for any insight into what our son was dealing with and how we could help him.

Benjamin had been texting with a high school student who was abusive and negative. As we considered the time stamp of the texting conversation and his emotional responses in the hospital, it became obvious that the conversation had been emotionally harmful for our son. He should have ended the conversation, but he didn't.

At that time, I'm not sure he had the ability to walk away from such a conversation. This student was bullying and belittling him. As she criticized him, she also indicated that her views were the views of all the other students at school. We knew she didn't speak for everyone, but when we put ourselves in Benjamin's place as an adolescent, it must have felt as if she did. We knew Benjamin struggled with relationships at school, but until we read the texting conversation, we hadn't understood just how much he struggled.

What should we do? Should we notify school officials about this conversation? School personnel had been very good at working with us to help Benjamin succeed. We knew he had issues to resolve, and he carried some personal responsibility. How should we address this inappropriate text? More significantly, how should we help him navigate through these struggles?

Benjamin was in the hospital overnight with what was again a manifestation of conversion disorder. Once again, he began regaining his mobility around lunchtime. He was discharged in the afternoon. By early evening, it was as if nothing had happened. Incidentally, he was still taking eight medications.

The weekend was good, but when Monday morning arrived, he refused to go to school. He didn't care what we did or said; it was as if our powers of persuasion had simply dissolved. No way was he returning.

Benjamin suggested home schooling. With the ongoing battles around the household, we knew we didn't have enough reserve to fight that battle too. We met with his pediatrician and then his therapist on that day, Monday, January 10. "The parents can't take it anymore," Dr. Padgett wrote in Benjamin's chart. That pretty much summarized where we were.

How our life had changed in just over a year.

Benjamin had always been in the top 2 percent of his class. Now he struggled academically. I had a new empathy for parents who labor to get their children to study and apply themselves in school. We'd never questioned whether Benjamin would attend college or not. Though he had always been a straight-A student, now we weren't concerned about good grades; we wondered if he'd be able to complete high school. Our task was to help him somehow receive a high school diploma. It wasn't simply a matter of grades. It was a combination of completing the work, managing the stress, dealing with relationships, and being able to function in a social environment.

I called two United Methodist–related facilities in Indiana that have residential programs for troubled teens. I had no idea whether these programs would be a fit for Benjamin's needs, but I had to find an option. Dr. Padgett also gave us the name of an out-of-state program that worked with adolescents with emotional issues. We could hardly bear the thought of sending our only child away from home at the age of fourteen, but we were out of options.

After Benjamin's pediatrician and therapist consulted with their office colleagues and talked with one another, they suggested we first try something less extreme: instead of placing Benjamin in a residential program, why not try an intermediate step of simply changing high schools? Changing school systems was a less radical step than many of our other possibilities. However, it would mean driving him to school and picking him up every day.

We studied and considered all the school systems within thirty miles of where we lived. Benjamin suggested that he transfer to Delphi, fourteen miles away. Whenever we'd been asked to move as I changed pastorates, the quality of the schools was one of the first things we ask about the community. We weren't moving, and now the only thing that concerned us about a new high school was whether Benjamin could have enough success to receive a diploma. He had lost so much control. If he wanted a fresh start at Delphi, we'd do what we could to help him succeed.

We didn't live in the district where the high school was located, but Delphi was willing to accept Benjamin, and his current school district was willing to release him. While his current school district had done everything they could to help Benjamin succeed, we knew they must have been relieved when he transferred.

Since he was changing schools, we chose not to address the texting issue. The texting exchange had been the proverbial straw that broke the camel's back. It had caused us to realize Benjamin needed a drastic change. Granted, we should've done a better job monitoring his texting and use of social media. Because we were dealing with so many other issues, that one had fallen through the cracks. Now, though we didn't read his texts, through our cell phone provider, we limited Benjamin's time texting. We blocked certain numbers to send to or receive from, and we could view a log of everyone with whom he communicated.

As a pastor of a local church, I'd always assumed my child would attend the local school. I believe it's important for a pastor and his or her family to be involved in the community where they serve, so Benjamin attending school in another community concerned me. Would he be shunned as an outsider? Would our community feel betrayed or snubbed if we sent our son somewhere else?

Fortunately, Benjamin was welcomed in Delphi. Most in our community respected our decision to help Benjamin get a fresh start. However, one person in the community believed she was giving Bootsie a reality check. She wasn't offended that we were sending Benjamin to a school in another community, but she shook her finger in Bootsie's face and said, "Your child is mentally ill. He needs to be locked up in an institution." We rejoiced that this person wasn't responsible for our son's medical or psychiatric care.

Benjamin was still emotionally fragile. He tired more easily than most, but he was determined to make the most of this fresh start. He didn't want anyone to know about his journey with GBS. He felt GBS and all of the twists and turns of his encounter with it had defined who he'd become in his last school. No way did he want that to happen again. If he ever felt weak or experienced the conversion disorder at school, he wouldn't let anyone see him in a wheelchair.

Benjamin started with a clean slate at Delphi, and he was a different kid. There'd been too much baggage at his last school. Some of the baggage was self-inflicted, but maneuvering through the many facets of his long recovery, he'd never been able to reestablish himself.

It had been over a year since he'd attended a full week of school. Once at Delphi, he missed only two class periods the whole semester, and his first absence was after about two weeks.

One day, a student came up to him at lunch and said, "I have a cousin who attended your last school. He said they all thought you were faking being sick."

Benjamin didn't defend himself or make excuses. Instead he replied, "That was in the past, and I really don't want to talk about it."

In his afternoon classes, he began having anxiety about the lunch conversation. He felt his legs begin to lock up. He went to the nurse's office, and I picked him up before the last period of the day. The next day he was fine.

The other class he missed was his first-period English class. It was a month into the semester, and he had a writing assignment. Other students in the class had had this teacher during the first semester, and they knew how she wanted things done. Benjamin either didn't know or didn't understand the necessity of doing things a certain way. The teacher informed him what he'd done wrong and reduced his grade. He was to resubmit the assignment.

When he got up that morning, he didn't want to go to school. This was unusual, because since transferring to Delphi, he'd regained his desire to attend. Finally, Benjamin shared what had happened in the previous English class. He didn't want to face the stress of first-period English. With extreme persistence, we got Benjamin in the car to go to school.

We arrived late, and he refused to get out of the car. I went in to talk with his guidance counselor. She and the school nurse were the only ones at the new school who knew the details of his health and emotional history. The English teacher had her prep period during second hour, so the guidance counselor suggested that the four of us—the English teacher, the guidance counselor, Benjamin, and I—sit down and talk.

I went to the car, and Benjamin agreed to be a part of the meeting. He understood the teacher's position and had accurately explained it to me. I believe the teacher might have extended some grace to him if she'd known more about his situation, but Benjamin didn't want her to know about his past. And he didn't want any grace or special considerations. He took the lower grade rather than risk repeating an experience of other students believing he'd received an unfair advantage. I was proud of him.

After a semester at Delphi, when he'd found his place as Ben Beeks, he did talk about his story with those who asked. Even though GBS had radically changed his life, he was no longer defined by it. He didn't miss any more school the rest of the semester. His grades, while not up to previous standards, put him on target for a high school diploma. Physically and emotionally, we were rising out of the dark to see the light at the end of the tunnel.

Epilogue

Benjamin discontinued the final medication related to all the physical and emotional twists and turns of his GBS journey in September 2011, twenty-two months after his diagnosis. We consider him fully recovered, but of course we have no way of knowing the long-term effects GBS will have on his overall strength.

At the time of diagnosis, he was prepubescent and five-foot, three inches tall. During his recovery, he grew seven inches. He is stronger now than he was at the time of diagnosis, and he's made the transition from being a boy to becoming a young man.

In December 2010, his counselor asked him if anything good came out of his bout with GBS. He said the only good thing was that his father had started running and was in better physical condition. I did run the One America 500 Festival Mini-Marathon in 2011, 2012, and 2013. Benjamin ran the 5K race again in 2011 and the mini-marathon in 2012 and 2013. He also ran cross-country and track his last three years of high school.

Five years after his diagnosis, Benjamin's reflections are more positive. While not wanting to relive those months, he likes who he has become and what he has learned through his encounter with GBS. He recognizes that he wouldn't be who he is today if he hadn't experienced it. Even though he's generally pleased with the growth he's experienced, he regrets the way he treated some people along the way. Some relationships are repaired. Others may never be.

Bootsie and I marked one culmination of our journey in September 2011 when Benjamin stopped his last medicine. He recognized the significance of that marker, but April 2012 was when he would mark the end. He identifies that date as the time he could say, "It's okay." It's okay that he had GBS. It's okay that he changed schools. It's okay that friendships changed. It's okay. Life goes on, and he's made the best of it.

Our journey as a family has made Bootsie and me more empathetic and compassionate toward families walking through difficult times. Life isn't easy, and none of us is exempt from problems and heartache. We are very pleased with the young man our son has become. However, we would never want to relive our GBS journey. Still, we recognize that the very journey we don't wish to relive has shaped him into the person we appreciate and love.

A faith lesson for all of us has been forgiveness. There were those who unintentionally hurt or disappointed us. We must release the hurt and forgive them. They don't need to know they hurt us, but we must forgive. There were also those who intentionally said hurtful things. Whether they ever seek forgiveness or not, we must forgive them. There are also those we hurt on our journey. As we remember or become aware of the pain we caused, we need to seek reconciliation and forgiveness. Even after five years, the healing of forgiveness continues.

In Romans 8:28, the apostle Paul writes, "And we know that in all things God works for the good of those who love Him, who have been called according to His purpose." Paul didn't say that everything that happens is good, but that God can use it for good. We believe God has used this GBS journey for good in our lives. We hope our journey can be an encouragement to others struggling with GBS or another long-term illness.

Benjamin did receive his high school diploma in the spring of 2014. At the end of his freshman year, he was number thirty-two in his class. He graduated number seven. He found his place in the student body of the Delphi High School. We are grateful for the opportunities in academics and leadership he was afforded there. He went on to attend Purdue University in the fall of 2014.

In February 2015, Benjamin had a bad case of intestinal flu. Even after his recovery from the flu symptoms, he said he didn't feel right. A week after recovering, he was admitted to the hospital once again with what we feared was a relapse of GBS. His symptoms were much less severe, but he was in the hospital for six days. He dropped one class, moved home for two weeks, and then returned to campus to finish his semester.

Relapses are rare. Depending on the source, it's estimated to be 3 to 5 percent. Although doctors are learning more about GBS through research, there is no way to predict or prevent its onset or a relapse. In an attempt to do what we could to minimize the chances of future relapses, in the summer of 2015, we took Benjamin to see a neuromuscular specialist at the Washington University of St. Louis Medical School. We chose Washington University because of their research and reputation as being one of the top hospitals treating GBS patients.

In the summer of 2015, it was impossible to recreate the symptoms that Benjamin had experienced earlier in the year, but the neurologist believed it was likely that he had experienced something called recrudescence instead of a relapse. A recrudescence happens when people have had GBS or some other disorder that has caused permanent neurological damage. Over time, they have a level of recovery. As they regain strength, the neurological damage is masked. Following a case of the flu or an infection, the neurological damage manifests itself again. There is no new nerve damage, but because of the person's weakened physical state, it may seem there has been a recurrence or additional deterioration.

We will never know with 100 percent certainty whether Benjamin's experience in February 2015 was recrudescence or a relapse, but recrudescence seems to be a reasonable explanation of what was going on in his body. Washington University determined that there was no evidence of active GBS or CIDP present in his body at that time.

Benjamin has resumed his normal schedule as a college student. When he physically pushes himself too hard, his body signals through nerve pain or discomfort his need to rest.

Even though we still have questions that may not be answered with absolute certainty, we pray for good health. If there are future health concerns or challenges, we believe God will see us through.

I once believed that God's work in our lives was most evident when all hope was lost. Through our GBS journey, God has caused a change in my thinking. Now I believe his work in our lives is most evident when hope is all we have left.

The Lord has done great things for us, and we are filled with joy.
Psalm 126:3